Having served as *The Statesman's* Special Correspondent in South-East Asia and the Far East for five years, S. Nihal Singh is in a unique position to relate the story of the birth of Malaysia, Indonesia's confrontation policy, Singapore's unceremonial exit from the Federation, Soekarno's downfall and the implications of the concept for the countries involved and the rest of the world. This is a first-hand account of the dramatic developments surrounding Malaysia. Mr Nihal Singh questioned the leaders of Malaya, Indonesia, the Philippines, Brunei and Singapore and came to his conclusions after assessing the words and deeds of politicians and how they affected the peoples of their countries.

Mr Nihal Singh's main conclusion is that only in Maphilindo lies the salvation of Malaysia, Indonesia and the Philippines.

MALAYSIA—A COMMENTARY

MALAYSIA—A COMMENTARY

S. Nihal Singh

BARNES & NOBLE, Inc.
NEW YORK
PUBLISHERS & BOOKSELLERS SINCE 1873

First Published in the United States, 1971
by BARNES & NOBLE, Inc.

ISBN 389 04579 9

Published in India by
Associated Publishing House
New Market, Karol Bagh, New Delhi-5

PRINTED IN INDIA

PRINTED AND PUBLISHED BY R. K. PAUL FOR
ASSOCIATED PUBLISHING HOUSE, NEW DELHI-5

To
My Father

Preface

This is a first-hand account of the exciting story of the birth of Malaysia, its troubled infancy, Singapore's exit from the Federation and the consequences of the concept for the countries involved—Malaya (now Malaysia), Singapore, Indonesia and the Philippines.

As *The Statesman's* Special Correspondent in South-East Asia and the Far East for five years, I had the opportunity of assessing the joys and the sorrows Malaysia brought about, the sorrows ultimately outweighing the advantages the concept might have had.

I was based in Singapore, but travelled often to the other capitals to report on the moods of the countries involved and the motivations of their dramatis personae. I talked to the leaders of Singapore, Malaysia, Indonesia and the Philippines and to the Sultan of Brunei.

The value of the book is in recreating those tempestuous days. I have refrained from rewriting my impressions. The epilogue is an attempt to relate the past to the present. In so far as this account contributes to the understanding of a momentous event in South-East Asia, whose importance for India and the world hardly needs stressing, it will have served its purpose. It is an Indian account of an Asian happening.

I am grateful to *The Statesman* for permitting me to use material first published in it.

S. Nihal Singh

Contents

1962
REVOLT, STRIFE & ARGUMENTS

1

"Singapore was", said my friend with a sigh, recalling the naughtiness of a city which has been put into the strait-jacket by socialist-minded reformers.

Three years ago, the People's Action Party put an end to what goes under the name of yellow culture. Week-end journals which specialized in risque jokes mixed with Cantonese jargon rich in double meaning were banned; so were lurid representations of pleasure: books, magazines and a whole lot of obscene literature. Also, striptease, and activities on its periphery.

Those were the days of PAP the Reformer. Fresh from a heady victory at the polls, the party was determined to reform the world. Marx still cast his long shadow; what is now the very pink Barisan Socialist group was then inside the ruling party. As so often before, socialism first sought to capture the citadel of decadent culture.

Then came the split in the PAP, political squabbles and the Malaysia fever. Over the years, the PAP and its leaders have undergone a remarkable change. From a party which prided itself on being non-conformist, the PAP is now the epitome of propriety. PAP leaders today not only play golf but also sit sedately to watch test cricket.

In this evolutionary process, the old passion for reform has given way to a new passion for creation. Singapore has a Ministry of Culture and a common theme of the Minister of Culture is the creation of a new Malayan culture. The attempt is to mix the four streams of Chinese, Malay, Indian and Western cultures in equal proportions and produce the new brew of Malayan—or Malaysian—culture.

Cultural experiments apart, this island city State of 1.7 million people still bears the imprint of PAP reforms. For one thing, no juke-boxes play. Shortly after the PAP came to power, police swooped on pin-table and juke-box saloons and bars and silenced hundreds of juke-boxes overnight. There were protests; the 400 juke-box operators offered to play only classical music if their licences were restored, but to no avail.

What was at stake, according to the Government, was not merely the dissemination of juke-box culture—although the reduction in noise was tremendous and hence welcome—but the fact that juke-box saloons harboured young thugs and attracted students and the unemployed.

Next, the anti-vice squad went into action. Dozens of hotels were ordered to be closed on the ground that they had permitted their premises to be used for immoral purposes. Under the axe fell a 30-year-old hotel which was Chinatown's landmark. The red light districts were combed out; massage parlours which were, in many cases, little more than brothels, were closed except for the few with qualified staff. Films were more heavily censored. Gambling devices like the one-arm bandit were outlawed.

Old Singapore now is little more than a memory. People have learnt to live with the more discreet version of a once-naughty city. To the striptease dancers and the massage parlour girls and their associates, a ready solution of their difficulties offered itself by emigration to Johore Bahru, just across the causeway from Singapore. Being in the Federation of Malaya, Johore Bahru is immune to PAP's reforms and is still near enough the big city for custom.

Naughtiness has, of course, not disappeared from Singapore but it is indulged in more furtively; the risks of illegal pleasure are greater. Vice is no longer on tap, as it were.

Massage parlours have given way to bars employing hostesses. The hostesses wait on single or group male custom while at the same time providing them company. For this privilege, customers have to tip heavily or stand the hostesses drinks. The hostesses' companionableness usually stays within the bounds of law, although sometimes erring bars are brought to book and before the public eye.

The institution of funlands survives but it is today a pale copy of what it was in the more wicked days. The funlands now consist of great areas, open by night, where one may dance with hostesses or indulge in some shopping or witness tawdry versions of Chinese plays.

There are many Singapores, each almost exclusive of the other. The Chinese, who form the overwhelming number of the city's population, are themselves divided by their own clan associations and, what is now emerging as the more important distinction, the possession of wealth. Singapore has a sizable colony of Chinese millionaires who live their own lives complete with exclusive gambling clubs. These millionaires mix with the richer *towkays* (Chinese businessmen) but their paths seldom cross those of the poorer Chinese.

Singapore's Chinatown is a world on its own. Its smells and noises are as distinctive as they are piercing. The pavements of Chinatown are strung with roadside shacks, a large proportion of which are record shops with blaring loudspeakers playing the latest pops (juke-boxes are out, but not the gramophone). But the real world of Chinatown lives in the lanes and bylanes. Although open gambling has been rooted out, the law can do little to stop people determined to gamble from doing so furtively. And the world of secret societies is still very real and commanding, even though the police are more aware of its ramifications than in former days. Apart from indulging in petty thievery, intimidation and kidnapping for ransom, secret societies usually take mortal revenge only on other secret society members.

A third category of Chinese is a radical, politically-conscious individual. He has received his schooling in Chinese language schools—a fact which often limits his ability to find good employment. He is the Angry Young Man of Singapore's society and his anger, coupled with frustration, inclines him to Communism (officially outlawed) or its substitute, the Barisan Socialist Party.

Indians form a considerable population—about 130,000—and are also divided into their regional associations and guilds. A familiar sight in Singapore's streets is the Sikh watchman called, *jaga*, who has pretty nearly monopolized the trade. Unlike in their original homeland, the Sikhs in Singapore have acquired a reputation for frugal living and are also known for their extensive money-lending activities. In the latter field, they aroused the ire of the PAP, which clamped down stringest restrictions on the rather high interest rate charged by the *jagas*. The *jagas*' best customers were the civil servants and it used to be common knowledge that they were the most influential outsiders in the Government since their creditors dared not refuse their requests.

Malays again form a separate group although in Singapore, unlike in Malaya, they seem somewhat overwhelmed by the Chinese. With few exceptions, Malays live in exclusive Malay areas.

Among the major radical groups, Europeans form a rather considerable population. Britons are by far the largest group, chiefly in commerce and industry, although there is a large U. K. Commission in Singapore and also the offices of the British Commissioner-General for South-East Asia as well as the British naval and air force bases.

British clubs in Singapore still endeavour to maintain an atmosphere of Victorian respectability and calm. Some succeed in doing so to a remarkable extent; others have given up the struggle in the hurly-burly of a changing world.

With many of these Singapores the transient visitor will hardly come into contact. The island's fortune, and misfortune, lie in the fact that most short-term visitors have but one purpose: shopping. The island's free port status brings in many visitors and much money. The longer term resident has two distinct grouses on this score. Shop assistants are as a rule surly because people will make purchases anyway, and there are few facilities to have goods repaired because things are cheap anyway. Cheapness and surliness often add up to expense and frayed tempers.

2

In the sultry coolth of Singapore, an oblong island of 31.5 square miles, the air is thick with politics. Singapore is traditionally radical, traditionally tempestuous and traditionally commercial.

Life and politics are inextricably interwoven, as they are in other parts of South-East Asia. Only, in this island city State at the tip of the Malayan archipelago, politics acquire a larger-than-life connotation; the politicians have a flamboyance which goes well with the mixed social and economic setting.

It would be wrong to mock at the prima donna air politicians have in Singapore. Beyond the exaggeration and self-importance assumed by people and events, a tempest is blowing.

The tempest has been caused by a phrase and a concept: Malaysia. As the hour of decision draws near, the ferment increases. Threats and counter-threats fly in the air; the epithet Communist is hurled at the Opposition with increasing frequency.

Singapore's basic problem is that it is a small island sandwiched between Indonesia and Malaya. It depends for its livelihood on entrepot trade, on the services it has to offer. It has few industries, a growing population and limited space.

The composition of its population further complicates the picture. Nearly 80% of the island's 1.7 million people are Chinese; the rest are Malays, Tamils, Eurasians and Europeans.

It is accepted on almost all sides that Singapore cannot exist as an independent entity. Today the British base provides employment to 20,000 people and is a symbol of protection. Singapore was granted self-government in 1959, with Britain retaining defence, foreign affairs and "security".

Singapore is linked to Malaya by a causeway guarded by two sets of police and customs officials. The casual visitor driving into the Federation from Singapore is greeted with politeness and smiles. But political exiles cannot cross the causeway. Through the causeway passes Singapore's trade with the Federation. The island's water supply comes from across the causeway.

May 27, 1961 is a date the people of Singapore can never forget. On that day, at a luncheon given in his honour in Singapore by the Foreign Correspondents' Association, Tengku Abdul Rahman, the Malayan Prime Minister, proposed Malaysia. This Malaysia, he suggested, should comprise Malaya, Singapore, British North Borneo and Sarawak and Brunei.

This represented a change in the Tengku's attitude. There was a time not so long ago when the Tengku would have nothing to do with Singapore—for two principal reasons: the Chinese content of the island's population and its radical politics. With the bringing in of the Borneo territories as a counterweight to Singapore's politics and Chineseness, Malaysia was now acceptable to Malaya with certain safeguards.

The concept of Malaysia was known before the Tengku spoke. A Malaysian Sociological Research Institute has been in existence much before May last year. The significance of the Tengku's speech was that he broached the concept as a practical proposition, not that the concept was new. Leftists allege that the plan was, in fact, British inspired.

The Tengku has stated that the idea occurred to him when he heard of the discussions British officials of the Borneo territories had with their home Government on the formation of a federation of Borneo States.

The Tengku, indeed, secured quick British assent to the principle of Malaysia. On his part, he displayed flexibility in negotiating over the future of the British base in Singapore. For the Borneo territories, a commission would ascertain the wishes of the people.

In Singapore's discussions with Malaya on the terms of the merger (and Malaysia), it was understood all along that the Federation Government would not permit the Chinese to become an almost equal race with the Malays. A special arrangement, therefore, was worked out whereby the citizens of Singapore would not be citizens of the new Federation, but merely its nationals. They would elect 15 members to the proposed Malaysian House of Representatives, but could not stand for Parliament from the present Federation or even vote in new Federal elections outside Singapore. On the other hand, the people of the Borneo territories would enjoy Federal citizenship.

To make this discriminatory clause look less discriminatory, the present Federal citizens were made to have the same disability in Singapore. In practical terms, this has little meaning. But the Malayan Government offered concessions in other fields—Singapore would have autonomy in labour and education. This answered two fears. Labour laws in Singapore are more liberal than in Malaya and education—much of it naturally in Chinese—would not suffer by overzealous Malayization.

These proposals were accepted by the Singapore Assembly as a working basis for merger after tempestuous debates. The Government promised to hold a referendum on the merger.

A referendum Bill is being studied by a select committee and is expected to have a third and final reading in the Singapore Assembly this summer. But the Government has already given an indication of the type of referendum it wants to hold. All unmarked or "uncertain" ballot papers, for instance, will count as votes for merger. This is justified on the specious ground that the Communists might confuse the voters into spoiling their ballot papers. Also, much will depend upon the wording of the referendum. Few in Singapore expect that the people will be asked the straightforward question: Do you want merger or not?

Opposition to the Malaysia plan in Singapore is genuine. There is first the antipathy between the Federation and Singapore. Malayan politicians have often taken a condescending attitude to Singapore, treating it as a problem child. At other times, they have bluntly expressed their dislike of the brand of politics Singapore follows.

In Malaya, there is a suspicion of the Chinese, that in the ultimate analysis their loyalties are to mainland China. Chinese chauvinism, although espoused by only a minority in Singapore, has not helped to clear the air.

Nor have the Malays forgotten that almost all the Communists fighting the Government during the years of the Emergency were Chinese. The Malay peasant, in any case, is familiar with the Chinese middleman and there is no love lost between the two.

Although these attitudes of the Malays are understandable, they do not make acceptance of Malaysia the easier for Singapore. The Chinese respect and like the Tengku but they fear that his successors might not be as understanding and liberal, particularly in religious matters.

Apart from this mutual suspicion existing between the Chinese in Singapore and the Malays in Malaya, there are the terms of the merger. No amount of gloss put on by the ruling People's Action Party in Singapore can hide the fact that the citizenship clause is discriminatory to the people of Singapore.

The PAP has, indeed, said that the terms of the merger are not ideal, but they are the only practical basis on which the "inevitable union" with Malaya can take place at the present juncture.

The opposition Barisan Socialists, a breakaway group from the PAP formed in September last year as a protest against the party's politics, have been conducting an effective political campaign against the merger. They have described the merger terms as a sell-out and say that the people of Singapore would be second class citizens in Malaysia. The Barisan demands complete merger with full citizenship rights for the people of Singapore.

The PAP answer has been to smear the Barisan with the Communist brush. The Communist Party in Singapore is illegal, but it is a known fact that there are Communist sympathizers in the Barisan and there are similarities of approach—accidental or otherwise—between the Barisan group and the PKI (Indonesian Communist Party). The standard PAP argument is that the Communists oppose the Malaysia plan because they are not ready to take over Malaysia.

Whatever the truth in this allegation, the Leftists' conception of Malaysia is different in that they want Indonesia and the Philippines included in a future Malaysia and consider Indonesia as the heartland. In any case, Leftists cannot relish the obvious anti-Communist overtones of the Tengku's Malaysia and fear persecution in Singapore once it comes into being. But no political party objects to the concept of Malaysia although the concepts vary widely.

In a series of 12 masterly political broadcasts—now printed in book form in English, Chinese, Malay and Tamil—the Singapore Prime Minister, Mr Lee Kuan Yew, bared the "plot" of the Communists and traced his success in foiling a Communist takeover of the PAP. His account was complete with pseudonyms for Communist plenipotentiaries—called the PLEN—he had met. He sought to prove that the central figure of the Barisan Socialists, Mr Lim Chin Siong, is a Communist who takes his orders from senior underground CP leaders.

Mr Lim Chin Siong, to the Chinese man-in-the-street in Singapore, is still something of a martyr. And the Barisan arguments against the merger have caught on with the Chinese middle and working classes.

There is in Singapore a rather hard division between the so-called English-educated Chinese and the Chinese-educated Chinese. While the PAP has succeeded in convincing a number of Chinese in the first category that the merger is the only sensible solution for Singapore's problem, the bulk of the second category—who are the majority of the Chinese—are reportedly with the Barisan.

It is moreover unfortunate but true that the traditional prejudices between the different races have been heightened by the Malaysia debate. Both the PAP and the Barisan are accusing one another of employing communalism to win the battle. Racial riots have not been unknown in Singapore and many fear that the controversies raging round the Malaysia plan could spark off ugly communal disturbances.

The ultimate weapon in the Malaysia debate for the pro factions has always been the causeway. Used as a sword of Damocles over the heads of the people of Singapore, it has often been suggested that Singapore would be helpless if the causeway were closed. It has even been hinted that Malaya could cut off Singapore's water supply if the island were not sensible.

This ultimate weapon has been used twice by the Tengku in April. The Malayan Prime Minister has said that he would close the causeway by the end of the year if Singapore refused to accept merger and Malaysia. "Why shouldn't we close the causeway if keeping it open would present an easy access for subversive elements to enter and destroy our country?" asked the Tengku.

The Barisan has countered this warning by declaring that the closing of the causeway would harm the Federation more than it would Singapore. There is little doubt, however, that if the Federal Government took the extreme step of closing the causeway, it would bring greater misery to Singapore than to Malaya because the Federation is far bigger in size, resources and power. Malaya is Singapore's hinterland and 22% of the island's trade is with the Federation.

Malaya has been trying to build Port Swettenham to do away with its galling dependence on Singapore's modern port—so far with little success. Plans are also under way to build a new international airport in Kuala Lumpur.

For the tortured soul of Singapore, therefore, the choice is not easy. The Chinese have accepted with good grace the weightage in Malayan Government service given to Malays and they are taking a new interest in learning Malay, the national language of the Federation and of the Malaysia of the future.

The People's Action Party hopes that when the Chinese count their gains and losses—and the Chinese have a shrewd head for business—they will accept the merger that is being offered to them. Mr Lee Kuan Yew's target date for Singapore's merger with Malaya is June next year. Long before then, however, all the practical steps are proposed to be taken for a *de facto* merger.

Mr David Marshall, onetime Prime Minister and always a picturesque figure in Singapore's politics, has said that there could be no stability by "tricking the people of Singapore into an annexation with the Federation through a dishonest referendum".

A feeling is growing in Singapore that, in spite of the island's opposition to merger, the PAP will see it through.

3

Mr Lee Kuan Yew has the opposition in the State just as he wants it—divided and ruffled.

Under a new understanding with Tengku Abdul Rahman, he has announced, Singapore citizens would become citizens of Malaysia instead of being merely its nationals. Since the citizenship issue has been the major plank of the Opposition in its disapproval of the Malaysia plan, Mr Lee's announcement has produced many ripples.

Mr David Marshall has publicly stated that the new concession on citizenship seems to meet his party's demands. Another member of the Council of Joint Action, formed in June to oppose Malaysia, has suggested that the Council be dissolved now that its task had been completed.

The Barisan Socialists, on the other hand, continue to remain staunchly opposed to the Malaysia plan. The new concession its leaders describe, with some reason, as merely a change in name. They have asked voters to drop blank ballot papers in the referendum to be held on September 1.

Mr Lee's announcement certainly answers an emotional need of Singapore although it has come too late in the day—after the inequities of the merger proposals have been impressed upon the people by the opposition.

Nobody in Singapore is, however, talking about the real problem reflected in the merger agreement between Singapore and Malaya—the necessity of a mechanism to keep the racial balance between the Malays and Chinese in favour of the former. Granted this, Mr Lee has got as good terms for Singapore as any Prime Minister could have. But the referendum to be held will be less than fair to the opposition.

4

In between commercials advertising particular brands of cigarettes and face cream, Radio Singapore is broadcasting a jingle. It runs:

Unite through Merger and we will stand
Happy and free in one strong band.
Equal through Merger, citizens all,
Malaysia brings wealth to one and all.

There are prizes galore for writing stage and radio plays and songs on Malaysia. In the city streets are posters extolling the virtues of Malaysia—rather in the manner of face powder advertisements with their before and after use themes.

The full weight of an efficient, publicity-minded governmental machinery is geared to one concept and idea:

Malaysia. The referendum which will decide whether Singapore will merge with Malaysia is yet to be held. But there is little enthusiasm left for it; the nature and terms of the referendum are such that few have any doubt about its outcome.

The battle for merger is virtually over and the victor, by a long shot, is Mr Lee Kuan Yew. The Barisan Socialists and their associates have been outmanoeuvred.

The appeal to the U.N.'s Special Committee on Colonialism made by 19 opposition members of the Singapore Assembly was a last faltering shot. Mr David Marshall, the genius behind the move, had apparently himself hoped little, except perhaps publicity, from it. Whatever the deficiencies of the referendum—and there are many—the Bill to hold it has been passed by a duly elected legislature.

Even at the U.N. Mr Lee got the better of his opponents by reaching New York before them. By the time four members of the opposition team arrived, Mr Lee had swayed the majority of the committee's members to his side in informal discussions by his persuasive arguments and enthusiasm. Mr David Marshall, who could have given Mr Lee a good fight in debate, reached New York only when the debate was, to all intents and purposes, over although he made a gallant effort.

Mr Lee Kuan Yew's referendum ensures, as far as any referendum can, that the people of Singapore will agree to the merger proposals worked out between the Singapore and Malayan Governments. The other two choices given are: a "complete and unconditional merger" as a State of Malaya or to enter Malaysia on terms "no less favourable than the terms for the Borneo territories".

For the opponents of Mr Lee's merger, the second choice is even more unacceptable than the first since the autonomy given to Singapore in labour and education under the official merger proposals will be denied, without compensating advantages.

In rejecting the White Paper proposals on Malaysia, the opposition's theme song has been the pertinent point that after merger the Chinese vote will, in effect, be depressed. This has been done to prevent the Malay-Chinese ratio from tilting in favour of the Chinese—something the Malayan Government will not tolerate. The opposition, therefore, has been demanding full merger—knowing that Malaya will not accept it.

Mr Lee has slanted this demand just a little to make it look ridiculous, because if Singapore would become another province of the Federation it would lose autonomy in labour and education as well as the citizenship of a number of the island's inhabitants—Malaya's citizenship laws are stricter than those under which citizenship was accorded to a large number of people in Singapore in 1957. What the opposition really demands is that all Singapore citizens should automatically become full-fledged citizens of the Federation on merger.

The third choice is hardly one of substance and was accepted by the People's Action Party to humour Mr Lim Yew Hock's Singapore People's Alliance, whose support has been invaluable to the PAP in the Assembly.

Voting in the referendum is compulsory and the only choice given to the electorate is to vote for one of the three alternatives. All "blank and uncertain" votes will be counted for the Government—surely a unique provision in any referendum held anywhere in the world.

Although Mr Lee justifies this clause on the ground that the Communists would otherwise wreck the referendum, he is here begging his question. Few in Singapore doubt that given a straight yes or no choice, the people of the island would vote against the merger proposals.

Why then hold a referendum at all, particularly when the PAP asserts that it was elected to power on the merger platform? For one thing, the Government had promised to hold one before finally accepting the merger terms. Secondly —and this is the more important reason—the interminable midnight debates on referendum in the Assembly and the airing of views in the Press have served the useful purpose of allowing the opposition to let off steam.

It is ironical that the Referendum Bill was passed by the Singapore Assembly shortly after the PAP became a minority Government–in August it held 25 seats in a House of 51. One of its members resigned while the referendum debate was in progress.

There are, however, weaknesses in the opposition case. It is well known that, given the present realities, the Malayan Government will not take in Singapore on the basis of full citizenship rights for the million and more Chinese on the island. The opposition arguments, practically speaking, therefore amount to a continuation of the semi-colonial status for Singapore—a point fully exploited by Mr Lee in New York. Also, the opposition spokesmen, particularly the trade union leaders among them, have spoken softly about the British military bases on the island since they provide livelihood to an embarrassingly large number of Singapore's labour force.

There are Communist sympathizers among the Barisan Socialists. It is, however, less certain whether all important members of the party are Communists and are guided by Communist Party policies. But in debate the fact that both the Communists and the Barisan Socialists oppose Mr Lee's merger has given the Prime Minister a convenient stick to beat the opposition with, and to gather support from the anti-Communist and non-Communist worlds.

What of the future?—presuming that things will go according to general expectations and Mr Lee's plans. Rumours of impending riots are ever present in Singapore but are less insistent at present. Indeed, the Barisan leaders have taken particular care to stress the constitutional aspect of their opposition to the merger proposals. The trade union leaders—an important segment of Singapore's political life—have been more expressive of the frustrated mood of the opposition.

India has come in for its share of brickbats from the opposition. India's sponsorship of the "no-cognizance" resolution in the U.N.'s Committee on Colonialism elicited a rebuke from Mr S. Woodhull. This trade union leader and a vice-chairman of the Barisan paid Mr Y.K. Puri, Indian High Commissioner in Kuala Lumpur, the compliment of making India's policy on Malaysia while describing him as the "golf-playing type". Mr David Marshall himself has described India's role in the U.N. committee as the "cruelest blow of all".

For the present, the opposition has no plan of voicing its grievances except through constitutional means even though the more extreme of the opposition leaders fear that their days of freedom are numbered. The Federation Government, which does not take a very liberal view of strikes or Communist sympathizers, is expected to give little leeway to the extremists in Singapore when the island becomes a part of Malaysia.

Although the opposition seems to have resigned itself to the Malaysia of Mr Lee's concept, it undoubtedly has its eye on long-term prospects. It can, for instance, hope to form the State Government in Singapore after Malaysia comes into being; there is little doubt about its popularity among the Chinese. Secondly, it can form an alliance with the opposition Socialist Front in the Federation, thus acquiring greater scope for its activities.

5

Ranging from the extreme Left to the extreme Right, political parties in Malaya are jostling with each other for a place in the sun in Malaysia.

Seldom has such political activity been witnessed in the five years of Malayan independence. Party headquarters are beehives of activity. New plans, new membership drives, new names and combinations are emerging as Malaysia draws near.

Party politics are of very recent origin in Malaya. They date from the end of the Second World War. Several mushroom parties then emerged on the scene, but it was the Union Constitution given to Malaya—later substituted by the present Federal Constitution—which brought forth Malay protests and the formation of the first major indigenous party: the United Malays National Organization.

Under the existing Constitution, which is to serve as the basis for the Malaysian Constitution, Malays enjoy special rights and privileges. (Malays are defined as indigenous Muslim people.) Similar privileges will also be enjoyed by the non-Muslim indigenous people of the Borneo territories in Malaysia.

The philosophy behind the Federal Constitution for Malaya, ultimately accepted by the British Government, is that Malays, being indigenous and by and large poor, deserve privileges to catch up with the Chinese and, to a lesser extent, the Indians.

These circumstances impinge upon all party politics in Malaya. By virtue of the Constitution, the Malays have become the dominant political factor (there is a four to one ratio in favour of Malays in Government service); the Chinese largely control the economy, to the extent it is not controlled by Western interests; Indians have done quite well for themselves in the professions, in spite of the fact that people of Indian origin are mostly labourers on rubber plantations.

Flowing from the racial divisions are the three main parties of Malaya: the United Malays National Organization, the Malayan Chinese Association and the Malayan Indian Congress. The three are clubbed together in an Alliance which forms the Government of Malaya.

Ranged against the ruling party are the Socialist Front comprising the Labour and Rakyat (People's) parties, the Pan-Malayan Islamic Party, the new United Democratic Party and the People's Progressive Party.

Racial tensions are never far from the surface of politics in Malaya. Mr D. R. Seenivasagam, a PPP leader, has aroused the ire of UMNO politicians by criticizing the special privileges of the Malays. Several UMNO groups were, in fact, planning to seek to deprive Mr Seenivasagam of his citizenship but the move was quashed by the party high command.

Tengku Abdul Rahman spoke about Malay rights at the 15th general assembly of UMNO in August in the following chilling sentences:

"As a matter of fact, the non-Malays live in better condition than the Malays. It can be said that they control the economy and commerce, and because of their high standard of living they are able to send their children to the universities in and outside the country, more than the Malays. What is left to the Malays is a little opportunity for earning their livelihood in their own country. We govern this country with justice and without confiscating other people's rights."

In the same address, the Tengku announced that UMNO's membership had topped the 100,000 mark. The new target for membership, to be attained by January next year, is 500,000. UMNO then is the dominant political organization of the Malays and the opposition it has met so far from within and without has not dented its strength.

The PMIP, which is vying with UMNO for Malays' support, has failed to fulfil its earlier promise and is largely a regional party, its stronghold being the State of Kelantan bordering on Thailand. Although a religious-oriented party of the extreme Right has an obvious appeal in a country which has a State religion (Islam), the temper of the Malays apparently does not suit this brand of politics.

Among the multi-racial parties seeking to win Malay favour is the Socialist Front. The SF has made some impressive gains but continues to suffer from a weakness shared by all Leftist parties in Malaya: lack of Malay support. As such, it can offer only limited opposition to UMNO in Malaya.

The People's Progressive Party has never got much beyond its stronghold in Perak State in the north-west although the two Seenivasagam brothers (one a Vice-President and the other the Secretary-General of the party) keep themselves in the public eye by their controversial speeches.

The United Democratic Party, which claims to be multiracial, is still an imponderable. It was formed in April and met with an impressive amount of attention from the other parties. Dr Lim Chong Eu, the brain behind the new party, is a former President of the Malayan Chinese Association and is a shrewd, capable and influential man. He has yet to show his hand; his party's objectives are general and unexceptionable.

That leaves the two junior members of the Alliance. The Malayan Chinese Association was formed in 1949 during the days of the Emergency to unite the community against the Communists and seek an improved status for the Chinese. It has now expanded into a large party of well-to-do and rich Chinese business men and traders although it also has in its ranks members of the professions.

The Malayan Indian Congress, set up shortly after the war and the last to join the Alliance, was subjected to some criticism at the UMNO conference in August in that it was not "pulling its weight" as a partner of the Alliance. There have, indeed, been some dissensions in the organization and a new effort is being made to energize the weak branches.

Against this background must be studied the new moves of the political parties to gain strength in Malaysia. It is inevitable that the racial texture of Malayan politics will be superimposed on Malaysia and it is therefore important to know the racial content of the new set-up. Malaysia will have a population of about 10 million with the following proportions for the three major races: 42% indigenous (including the tribes of the Borneo territories), 38% Chinese and 10% Indians (including a small proportion of Pakistanis).

An UMNO organization already exists in Singapore although Malays in the city State form a small proportion of the population. In the three Borneo territories which are to comprise Malaysia—North Borneo, Sarawak and Brunei—it is reasonable to expect that the Malays (some 180,000) will be potential membership material for UMNO.

The Malayan Chinese Association is sending one of its senior leaders to the Borneo territories to seek support—and members. There are about 335,000 Chinese spread over the three territories and some of them will no doubt rally round the MCA, a source of power and position.

The Singapore Malayan Indian Congress—not a branch of the MIC in Malaya—has been in existence for some time although a splinter group is trying to lead a different movement. Dato V.T. Sambanthan, the Malayan Works and Telecommunications Minister who has been re-elected National President of the MIC, was recently in Singapore to urge on the Indians the virtues of unity. The MIC Vice-President, Mr V. Manickavasagam, is charged with bringing the Borneo Indians (numbering only a few thousands) together under the MIC banner.

In normal circumstances, a proportion of the Chinese who call themselves socialist would belong to the Communist Party. But the 12 years of Emergency involving a relentless fight against Communist guerrillas has made the CP illegal. China, however, continues to be a powerful psychological factor in the thinking of the Chinese.

The MCA, being a party of the haves, can exercise but limited appeal for the poorer Chinese. Curiously, however, financial success is rated so highly by the overseas Chinese that prosperity makes them place business above ideology.

Leftists have fired the first shot by setting up a Malaysia Secretariat in Singapore. In some ways, Malaysia means a natural acquisition of strength for the Socialist Front of Malaya. It has the ideological support of the Barisan in Singapore as also of the Sarawak United People's Party and of Leftist groups in North Borneo and the tiny Sultanate of Brunei. In the last, the anti-Malaysia Rakyat Party made a clean sweep in the territory's first elections.

In practice, however, there remains the formidable task of reconciling individual and regional rivalries among the Leftists. And the Socialist Front, being the only Malayan party of some influence which cuts across racial barriers, is at the same time more susceptible to ideological rifts. If these weaknesses can be surmounted, the Socialists can provide powerful opposition to UMNO.

On the other hand, the Malayan Chinese Association has only recently proved its strength in the local council elections in Malaya. It helped the Alliance gain control of 215 local councils out of a total of 286 in eight States. The Socialist Front could get control over only 13 councils. Since 80% of the Alliance candidates were MCA Chinese, the Association can claim a significant victory. Nor is the MCA resting on its laurels. A big publicity drive is planned for Malaya and the organization is making a serious effort to woo the poorer Chinese voter. It has tremendous resources for its programmes.

For the immediate future, the United Malays National Organization need have no serious worries. The latest crisis in its affairs—caused by Mr Abdul Aziz bin Ishak resisting his transfer from the key Agriculture and Co-operatives Ministry—has been weathered by the Tengku with admirable agility. It is now clear that Mr Aziz, who enjoys considerable support among sections of Malay agriculturists, has been forced to take an anti-Tengku stand years before he was ready for it. The Tengku recognized the danger to UMNO presented by a Left-leaning Malay leader like Mr Aziz leading a popular Malay movement. He was equal to the occasion.

As a step forward, UMNO has opened associate membership status for non-Malays, a move that has not been universally popular with MIC members, for instance, because it would cut into their strength. But Tengku Abdul Rahman knows that as long as the Leftists fail to attract the mass of Malays, there is no real danger to the power and influence of UMNO. The Socialists are still a long way from achieving Malay support and no matter what parties have the support of the Chinese, it is the Malays who will call the tune in the political affairs of Malaysia.

6

Other than India's immediate neighbours, no third country has become so directly involved in the Sino-Indian border conflict as Malaya and Singapore. The conflict has become a live issue for every political party in the two territories.

Given the composition of Malaya's population, the clash would have inevitably posed problems for the country's political parties. With Tengku Abdul Rahman's repeated support for India—voiced during his visit to India in October and at home—the issue has become a national controversy. And the institution of an official Save Democracy Fund for India has forced many parties to take a public stand.

The major problem of Malaya—and the future Malaysia—is to weld the different races into one nation. Although Malaya's record of inter-racial peace is good (Singapore's, however, is not equally commendable), a Malayan consciousness is still far from pervasive. Emotional pulls exercise a powerful influence on Indians as they do on the Chinese.

It is therefore hardly surprising that two of the main races of Malaya and Singapore should find themselves emotionally on opposite sides in the Sino-Indian border conflict. But the Chinese are admittedly placed in an embarrassing position in view of their past protestations of loyalty to their adopted home.

There are no subtle undertones to Malaya's anti-Communism and the Chinese in Malaya have had to be equally forthright in their public condemnation of Communism. In Singapore, where the fashion is to lean to the Left, the political atmosphere permits of equivocation, but the People's Action Party for one has unreservedly accepted Tengku Abdul Rahman as the leader of the Malaysia region.

With the Tengku's characteristic and heartwarming reaction to the Chinese invasion of India, the gap between Chinese protestations and reality became gaping wide. Not being able to express their true feelings, the Chinese answered with silence. It took Singapore's Chinese language newspapers—normally keenly alive to world developments—more than two weeks to comment on the Tengku's stand. Malaya's basic stand—one of them ultimately commented—was to pray for a peaceful settlement of the border conflict.

The Tengku was not unaware of the implications of his support for India in the border conflict. Towards the end of his Indian tour, as on arrival in Singapore, he emphasized his view that the clash was not between Indians and Chinese but between Democracy and Communism. This enabled him to take the stand that he expected all Malayans irrespective of their race to support India, but it did not resolve the emotional problems of the Chinese.

Only the Tengku's United Malays National Organization could give uninhibited support to their leader. Members of the Malayan Indian Congress—elated over the Tengku's stand—were fearful of consequences. In Singapore particularly, the 130,000-strong Indian community felt psychologically beleaguered in a Chinese city. Collections for India's Defence Fund were therefore initially made quietly.

The Malayan Chinese Association—the third member of the Alliance—kept its thoughts to itself for the good reason that any public statement supporting India would have caused complications. It was only on the day the Tengku made a broadcast launching the Aid India Fund that Mr Tan Siew Sin, the MCA President, told members of his Association that if they viewed the Sino-Indian conflict putting Malaya's interest before everything else, they "cannot go far wrong". At the moment, however, it was a dispute which did not appear to concern them directly, he said.

In Singapore, Tengku Abdul Rahman's strong support for India produced an embarrassed silence from the People's Action Party. The PAP has many functionaries of Indian origin while there is the obvious pressure of Chinese opinion. Mr Lee Kuan Yew has only lately been trying to build himself up as a member of the non-aligned club and he could hardly afford to take a stand opposed to the Tengku's, with Malaysia in the offing. Till November 15, neither Mr Lee nor his party had expressed an opinion on the border conflict except to say that he was concerned with ensuring peace and harmony between the Indian and Chinese communities.

The Barisan Socialists were naturally less inhibited in viewing the Sino-Indian clash although the party has some important officials of Indian origin in the trade union wing. After a long silence, the party's Secretary-General, Mr Lim Chin Siong, declared that as Malayans they were not interested in the exact location of the McMahon Line and wanted peaceful settlement of all disputes.

Although most political parties have therefore had to take a public stand, if only to skirt the issue, individual Chinese have not felt the same restraints. In letters to newspapers, in speeches in town councils and elsewhere there have been dark references to possible undesirable consequences of Malaya taking sides in the border conflict.

In spite of these rumblings, the Tengku refused to water down his support for India. In a broadcast to the nation, he launched the Save Democracy Fund to help India while issuing the following warning—clearly directed at the Chinese:

"There may be Malayans who feel themselves involved in a racial conflict because of this trouble on the border rather than an ideological conflict. I say to them they are not true Malayans and all their protestations of loyalty to this country as Malayans is all false and nonsense."

The warning stung, and produced a "cascade of letters" which were commented upon but not published by a leading

Singapore and Kuala Lumpur newspaper. Chinese newspapers in Malaya answered with silence. A leader of the Chinese-based People's Progressive Party retorted: "The most alarming statement made by the Tengku is to suggest that all those who oppose donations for India are not loyal to this country. This is most fantastic and annoying to large sections of the people of Malaya."

The Socialist Front of Malaya has gone a step further in charging the Alliance Government with using the border dispute "for communal party propaganda, with the aid of the reactionary Press". This cry of communal harmony in danger has ironically been serving both the extreme Left and the extreme Right among the Chinese-based parties.

The first big donation—of M$ 15,000—to the Save Democracy Fund came from readers of a Tamil newspaper in Kuala Lumpur. Other Indian residents and associations have been sending in their contributions, but several days after the Fund was launched by the Tengku it had not reached even the modest M$ 50,000 mark. This is not impressive in a country where people are both quick and generous with giving money for a good cause and is plainly due to the fact that the richest community is not enthusiastic about it. Not so long ago, a newspaper appeal for a Chinese schoolgirl who had lost both arms in a road accident yielded well over M$ 100,000.

7

The royal washing was spread out on the first floor balcony of Brunei Town's Secretariat building. Two of the Sultan's eight children were playing hide and seek amidst office files. A cardboard notice propped up on a chair in the balcony announced: The private apartment of His Highness.

A stone's throw away, scores of rebel prisoners sat on the floor of Brunei Town's main police station. They looked like ordinary Malay folk—adequately clothed and well-fed—except for an inscrutable sad expression on their faces. They had just received square paper parcels of food—boiled rice and a dash of curry—and some of them began to peck at them gingerly.

Outside, on the main grassy square of Brunei Town, a Royal Navy helicopter was ferrying British officers from the centre of town to HMS Albion. A European lady resident of Brunei was at the wheel of her parked car waiting to see the machine lift itself like an outsized monkey. The helicopter made a glorious picture against the large white rotundity of the town's landmark, the Saifuddin mosque; as if called by a photographer's wish, clouds floated by in the background. The lady excitedly clicked her camera and explained to an amused Tommy standing around: "You know, this has never happened before in Brunei."

For long the tiny Sultanate, wedged in between North Borneo and Sarawak, was known for piracy and little else. Oil was first discovered in 1929, but before it could be exploited commercially in large quantities, the war intervened. After the war oil production soared and brought in big money.

Brunei's population of around 84,000 benefited. Some benefited more than others. The 47-year-old Sultan, Sir Omar Ali Saifuddin, began a programme of development—mainly as a device to spread the State's opulence a bit. Major development came to a halt about four years ago; so did Shell's expansion, in view of declining oil production.

As the Sultan proudly claims, there are no needy persons in his State. The contraction of public and private development expenditure merely meant that the shops had rather less custom. The Malay who did not find a ready job went back to his *kampong* (settlement) to subsistence farming.

Some of the glittering prizes of oil wealth are still available to the Brunei resident. There is no income tax on individuals. The State provides extensive medical benefits and old age pensions. A programme of Bruneization means that the local man has a great advantage in securing jobs. The State's accumulated funds stand at the respectable figure of M$ 769 million; the annual revenue surplus is in the region of M$ 80 million.

In 1958 Brunei's first—and until recently sole—political party was registered. The Rakyat Party was—and is—a Malay party. Malays constitute about half of Brunei's population; the only other numerous community is the Chinese (over 21,000). Gradually, the Rakyat Party built its following—spreading its socialist ideas with a dash of romanticism. This romanticism consists of working for a union of the three Borneo territories under Brunei's leadership. Since Brunei once ruled all of Sarawak and most of North Borneo, this concept naturally exercises a fascination for the prince and peasant in Brunei.

Mr A.M. Azahari quickly became the undisputed leader of the Rakyat Party. He is a born orator and the amalgam of his silver tongue and Malay susceptibility to eloquence produced a devoted following. Mr Azahari's own Indonesian orientation—he fought against the Dutch with Indonesian guerrillas—inclined him more to Indonesia than to any other country. In any event, Malaya's particular brand of parliamentary democracy coupled with free enterprise holds little attraction for the Malay intellectual abroad.

Mr Azahari worked for his ideals within the context of the people's loyalty to the Sultan. Apart from his own connexions with the Brunei aristocracy—this is not difficult when viewed against the size of the entire Malay population in Brunei—Mr Azahari believed that he had interested the Sultan in this project. How far the Sultan encouraged the Rakyat Party leader in this belief is still unknown.

The rebellion, which began in the early hours of December 8, has raised more questions than it has provided answers for. It is fairly well established that a prime objective of the revolt was to stem Malaysia, but many circumstances and trends merged to produce it.

It seems clear that the rebels had to speed up their plans in view of the arrests made by the police in Lawas—the Sarawak territory adjoining Brunei—a week before the rebellion started. Among the documents captured from the rebels are plans indicating an organized system of command. On the other hand, the rebels used the most rudimentary arms—largely shotguns and a few rifles—to wage their battle.

The sudden emergence of uniforms with the buffalo head—the Rakyat Party symbol—also indicates preparation. There is now pretty firm evidence that a certain amount of drilling with wooden rifles was undertaken by the rebels in jungle areas.

The 500 or so rebels arrested—many more are under detention—are almost entirely taking the line that they were misled. While they are thereby attempting to minimize their role in the revolt to escape punishment, the line fed to the rank and file by the Rakyat Party leaders (the "North Borneo National Army" is a closely allied arm of the party) was that the British would not intervene and that help from outside in men and material would be forthcoming. Some of the rebels were told specifically that help would arrive from Indonesia and the Philippines.

Except for a small and very privileged minority, almost the entire adult Malay male population of Brunei would seem to have participated in the revolt, directly or otherwise. The rebels include a large number of Government employees as also Shell employees at the Seria oilfields (the general secretary of the newly-formed Oil Workers' Union in Seria is a Rakyat Party leader). For its own survival, the Brunei Government will therefore be forced to accept most rebels' statements of being misled at face value.

I asked the Deputy Mentri Besar (Deputy Chief Minister) of Brunei, Dato Pengiran Ali, during an interview what he thought of this feature of the revolt. He said the Government employees who took part in the revolt (significantly, the official interpreter first spoke of the "revolution", quickly correcting himself) were drivers and daily-rated labour, thus unwittingly giving it a classic Marxian ring.

Dato Pengiran Ali is the Sultan's closest adviser and his appointment a few months ago produced an outcry from the Rakyat Party which felt that the post should have gone to one of its supporters. Among others surrounding the Sultan are the Mentri Besar (Chief Minister), Dato Marsal. During half an hour's interview I gathered the impression that he felt unsure of his ground; his activities, in any case, continue to be something of a mystery. He is not a born Brunei citizen—his father came from Sarawak—and he was apparently converted to Islam.

Both Dato Marsal and his deputy are founder members of the Brunei Teachers' Association. A third founder member is the Assistant State Secretary and Director of Broadcasting. This preponderance of teachers among the Sultan's advisers is largely due to the fact that secondary education came to Brunei only in the early fifties and teachers therefore had a good start in the administration.

The Sultan himself is a devoted family man. He lives very modestly in spite of the State's wealth and has taken only one wife. He draws a privy purse of only M$ 150,000 a year from State revenues; the 1961 Budget surplus amounted to over M$ 81 million. The Sultan, it would seem, listens to his advisers and it is perhaps because of this that the advisers have been able to fend off all outsiders from positions of power. However, the Sultan's own predilection to continue to remain a reigning monarch is well known.

Mr Azahari, in any event, seems to have been prevented from acquiring power. The London talks over Brunei's new Constitution did not include any Rakyat Party representative. After the elections to the district councils in which the Rakyat Party made a clean sweep, the appointment of a Deputy Mentri Besar was interpreted by it as a slap in the face. (The Brunei Government claims that this appointment was, in actual fact, made before the elections, but there are grounds to doubt the veracity of this statement.)

Brunei's first written constitution was negotiated in London in April, 1959. It came into force in September that year and the aim of the constitutional agreements was to revise Brunei's relationship with Britain, end Sarawak's resented dominance in the State's administration and lead Brunei to a more democratic form of Government. Britain's Resident in Brunei became a High Commissioner although London continued to be responsible for defence, external affairs and internal security.

Under the Constitution, the Sultan can exercise supreme executive authority and it does not follow from the Rakyat Party's success in the district council elections (which enabled it to capture all the 16 elected seats in a Legislative Council of 33) that it should have its members in the administration. It is, however, clear that if the only political party of proven popularity is not represented in the Government's executive apparatus—as was the case—things had reached a sorry pass.

Although according to the London agreement of 1959 the Sultan is bound to accept the British High Commissioner's advice on all matters except religion and Malay custom, the British have exercised minimal control over the protectorate. This is due as much to the practical difficulties of exercising tight control over a protectorate in these days of vanishing colonies as to complacency in British circles in Brunei and elsewhere. Apart from the complete failure of British intelligence to read the signs of revolt, British administrators in Brunei had apparently been living in an unreal world and took the social graces of the Rakyat Party leaders for a guarantee that they would play the parliamentary game in Brunei according to British rules.

A key part of the London agreement of 1959 is Britain's right to intervene in Brunei in times of a "grave internal menace to the peace or tranquillity of the State". Although this right is absolute in exceptional circumstances, a possible British intervention without the Sultan's invitation would have proved politically embarrassing for Britain. It was possibly in the hope that Britain might not intervene in those circumstances that the rebels sought to keep the Sultan with them.

The Brunei constitution has been in force since September, 1959, but at least two of the seniormost officers of the Sultan's Government appeared to have only a rudimentary knowledge of it. In the post-rebellion week, in any event, the constitution was of mere academic interest. The constitution was made to suit decisions instead of decisions being made in the spirit of the constitution. The Sultan's advisers —as indeed some British experts—seemed overwhelmed by the rebellion.

By itself, the rebellion would have amounted to a "storm in an oil barrel", as was suggested by a wag. It is characteristic of South-East Asia that the ripples of the Brunei affair have travelled far and wide.

Such was, in any event, the aim of Mr Azahari's Rakyat

Party, and if Mr Azahari has not succeeded in internationalizing the conflict, he has regionalized it.

Relations between Indonesia and Malaya—seldom cordial in recent years—have reached a new low. Protest notes and warnings are flying back and forth between Kuala Lumpur and Djakarta. The Philippines—whose claim to North Borneo has been ignored by Britain—took particular delight in entertaining Mr Azahari in Manila, thus providing him with an invaluable propaganda base. But President Macapagal has wisely stopped short of the brink, and official support has not been given officially to Mr Azahari.

The significance of the Brunei revolt lies in the fact that the British protectorate is one of the five territories proposed to be grouped together in Malaysia by August next year. Malaya is the only really keen member of the proposed Federation. Singapore was made to agree to Malaysia through a referendum which was nothing of the kind.

The British territories of Sarawak and North Borneo have been made to agree to Malaysia through various means. Only the tiny Sultanate of Brunei was prevaricating. The place to strike therefore was Brunei; the time, before Malaysia irrevocably came into being.

There were two distinct urges for the revolt, both of them anti-Malaysian. Whatever hopes Mr Azahari entertained of achieving power in Brunei would have been frustrated by Malaysia. The hands of the Sultan of Brunei's advisers would have been strengthened by the dominance of Kuala Lumpur and the Right-wing Alliance Government of Malaya could be expected to come down heavily on all Leftist groups and forces in Malaysia.

For the anti-Malaysia groups in the other two Borneo territories, as also in Singapore and Malaya, the strength of the Rakyat Party and the Sultan of Brunei's prevarication were a heaven-sent opportunity to try to wreck Malaysia. Brunei's most valuable gift was that the Rakyat Party was a truly Malay organization. With a Chinese-based party, a rebellion would have failed before it could have been launched.

There were extensive contacts and consultations between Mr Azahari and leaders of Leftist parties in Sarawak, North Borneo, Singapore and Malaya. At least some Filipino leaders and members of the Indonesian Communist Party were also taken into confidence.

Although the revolt probably had to be advanced because of the arrest of rebel leaders in Sarawak, plans to strike simultaneously in the three Borneo territories were carried out. It was largely due to the rebels' inadequate preparation that British and Gurkha troops could contain the revolt in its early stages in Brunei and a semi-circular belt around it.

There is some evidence to suggest that Indonesians, as individuals or representatives of political parties, took a hand in the revolt. Rebels' statements that they were told Indonesia would come to their help are not, by themselves, proof of Indonesian involvement.

However, in the oil town of Seria I was told by one of the two Indian hostages kept by the rebels that he was ordered to control Indonesian and Philippine planes coming in. The Indian in question, Mr T.J. Joseph, who is the senior air traffic controller at Seria's Anduki airport, could have had little purpose in fabricating such a story.

Also in Seria, several old residents said they had never seen some of the rebel leaders before—and Seria is a small town. Although Dutch evidence is suspect, an interesting point made to me by a Dutch engineer in Seria was that some of the rebel leaders spoke the Indonesian variety of Malay—Bahasa Indonesian.

Indonesian leaders, from President Soekarno down, have now given full moral and ideological support to the rebels. It is, however, important to distinguish between Indonesian sentiments—violent as they may be—and actuality. On the other hand, it is only fair to assume that if an Indonesian political party smuggles arms or leaders into the pirate-ridden waters of Borneo, the Indonesian Government would close its eyes. Some parties—perhaps the Indonesian Communist Party—may have actually done so. Indonesia has never been enthusiastic about sharing a land frontier with Malaya, which the Malaysia grouping will bring about.

Gun-running may also have been indulged in by some Filipino politicians—smuggling, at any rate, is a normal and traditional form of trade between the Sulu islands of the Philippines and the Borneo territories. But the Philippine Government would not willingly involve itself with such gun-running in view of the wider implications of the conflict.

For Malaya the rebellion in Brunei has come as a great shock. For one thing, it has knocked the bottom out of Tengku Abdul Rahman's main premise. Malaya has been particularly keen on bringing in the Borneo territories in Malaysia in order to use them as a counterweight to Singapore's Chinese and radical content. The rebellion has proved that at least one of the three Borneo territories is as infected with radicalism as the proverbially radical Singapore.

A particularly bitter pill for Malayans to swallow is that their brother Malays should have chosen to take up arms against a Federation which would have brought them closer to Malaya. However, there has for long been an undercurrent of anti-Malaya feeling in Brunei which has erupted into violence from time to time.

But Malaya's relations with the Brunei Government remain close in certain fields. Brunei's State Secretary is a

Malayan; so is the State's Attorney-General, who had a nervous breakdown a week after the revolt. Malaya also gives facilities to Brunei students. The Sultan himself was educated in Malaya and two of his children, including the Crown Prince, are studying there.

The Sultan of Brunei has reportedly been pressing for his right to be elected Malaysia's future Paramount Ruler —a privilege which is proposed to be restricted to Malaya's provincial rulers—before his State joins up. His bargaining position has been weakened by the revolt, although it would be wise for Malayan leaders not to try to obtain the Sultan's allegiance too cheaply. (Significantly, the Sultan has made no derogatory reference to Mr Azahari.)

Malaysia, in any event, will probably come into being by August next year—with much less alacrity than before the revolt.

1963
CONFRONTATION AND PEACEMAKING

8

No one who visits Indonesia can remain entirely uninfluenced by the enthusiasm that prevails in many fields of activity in this young republic of several thousand islands.

Indonesia obtained her independence through a revolution. No inquiring visitor is permitted to forget this; the process of winning freedom by having had to fight for it has been elevated to a cult. Indonesians believe that they have been tempered like steel by this struggle; no effort is, psychologically, too great for them.

In this heady atmosphere, political ideas and attitudes take shape which can be related only to this cult. Revolution has never had a stop in Indonesia. After independence—by no means a cut-and-dried affair—were the rebellions of one sort or another and the irritatingly persistent activities of the Darul Islam. It was only in January that the last 17 of the Darul Islam rebels surrendered; there was a ring of pride in Brigadier-General Adjie's voice as he related to me the last surrenders in Bandung.

Above all, the flame of Revolution has been stoked by the West Irian issue. Time and again the Dutch have played their part in making Indonesia more revolution-minded than necessary.

It is one thing to pass through a difficult time on the crest of enthusiasm; but even the most tireless human spirit tires of revolutions. It has therefore been the particular objective of Indonesia's rulers to give a new dimension to the word. Instead of a short tempestuous affair, the Revolution, to Indonesian minds, represents a continuous and continuing process of change—desired and secured by will and, if necessary, by force.

This indoctrination has been partially achieved by the propagation of slogans and concepts. Manipol, the Political Manifesto of 1959, is a household word in Indonesia. So are Marhaenism, the idealistic concept of benefiting the mass of the Indonesian people; gotong-rojong, the process of voluntary mutual co-operation in Indonesian communities now sought to be projected on a national and political scale; musjawarah, the holding of discussions in a spirit of reaching unanimity—the hard edges of opposing views are presumed to be rounded off in discussion.

In part, some of these concepts represent a desire to dig into indigenous norms of political philosophy—a predictable phenomenon in developing countries. Indonesia's contribution to this field of political activity has been the extent to which it has taken political indoctrination without having had to resort to a Communist State structure.

At the apex of the political concepts—broadcast and re-broadcast a thousand times—is Panch Sheel (Pantjasila to Indonesians) which has been developed into the national concept. The five principles stand for: Belief in God, Humanity, Nationalism, Sovereignty of the People and Social Justice.

The development of new concepts follows a somewhat predictable course. In most cases, President Soekarno sets the ball rolling; it is like dropping a pebble into a pool. The ripples are spread further afield by the State propaganda apparatus—at present headed by that most stimulating conversationalist, Dr Roeslan Abdulgani—and by the various political groups, each of which has its own particular axe to grind. The Indonesian Communist Party (PKI), for instance, manipulates concepts for its own party needs—an aspect of the situation which weighs heavily on Western experts in Djakarta.

The PKI then is by no means alone in manipulating slogans, but it is most adept at doing so—something to be expected from a Communist Party. Other parties try to do their bit for themselves by propagating the slogans that suit them. In this context, the Armed Forces should also be taken as a political party—they are trying to develop their own slogans.

In such an atmosphere of political thought, words such as colonialism, neocolonialism and imperialism acquire a purity and simplicity which they have ceased to enjoy in other parts of the non-Communist world. To an average Indonesian, colonialism is a symbol of evil, and he is inclined to think of himself as one fighting on the side of the angels. He is more than repeating a cliche when he expresses his indignation against colonialism; he is offering himself symbolically to the angels.

President Soekarno's two remarkable achievements are that he has given the Indonesian people a sense of national identity and pride and that he has kept thousands of scattered islands together as one nation. A glance at the map is sufficient indication of the difficulties presented by Indonesia's geography; taken together with the differences and suspicions that exist between one island and another and the complications of covert foreign aid in inflaming rebellions, the achievement of keeping Indonesia together is a valuable one.

The other achievement is equally impressive. The *betja* driver (the *betja* is a cycle rickshaw and is Djakarta's main means of public transport) is proud of Hotel Indonesia—a symbol of new Indonesia—although he knows that he cannot deposit his customers in the hotel compound, much less entertain there. Even while intelligent Indonesians express doubts about the wisdom of spending over U.S. $ 117 million on building the Asian Games stadium when the money could have been utilized for more utilitarian ends, they are proud that Indonesia owns a most modern complex of sports stadia.

This pride in Indonesia's accomplishments has brought complications (Indonesians tend to be extremely sensitive to criticism, even when it is meant well), but it has served to give the people a national identity. The Sumatran and the Javanese, for instance, remain very conscious of each other's differences which still greatly influence politics in Djakarta, but they share a common pride in being Indonesian.

While these two positive aspects of the Indonesian picture cannot be over-emphasized, they have brought in their wake their peculiar problems and left others unresolved. One limitation to propagating slogans is that it tends to encourage emotional attitudes which are hard to put aside. An average Indonesian is very willing to fight against colonialism, but less prone to reason about the nature or the implications of the fight in which he is participating.

In Djakarta I met one of the leaders of a political party which has been in the forefront in sending protest delegations to the British Embassy on the Brunei issue. This gentleman—a most likeable and charming man—had the vaguest notions about Brunei. Also in relation to Brunei, student groups were urging India to dissuade Gurkha troops from fighting in Brunei; only after a few days was it discovered that the Gurkhas' homeland is Nepal, not India.

It is also open to question whether the set of slogans and concepts made popular in Indonesia do not—of their own momentum—incline the country to attitudes and values which are contrary to President Soekarno's aims. Together with the helping hand extended by the PKI, a natural Indonesian tendency to side against the West on several issues can become accentuated. Many Indonesians are aware of this problem and it would be unwise to draw hasty conclusions from individual statements of Indonesian leaders, who are themselves somewhat conditioned by the slogans they propagate.

A more immediate and urgent problem before Indonesia is how to translate slogans and concepts in terms of digging channels and getting on with economic development. Here the psychological barrier to a rational assessment is formidable. Having been fed on the concept of a continuing revolution, the Indonesian mind is not conditioned to think of the more mundane tasks of economic development. While the present political concepts have served to give the people an Indonesian identity, they have at the same time served as an opiate. Only a gigantic effort initiated at the top and propagated through the various political layers to the people can start Indonesia on the road of sound economic development.

In terms of conventional economics, Indonesia's situation is desperate. The value of the Indonesian rupiah fluctuates like a weathercock on the open market—to an extent that Djakarta's Hotel Indonesia accepts payment from foreign guests only in foreign currency. Production in the nationalized enterprises (the former Dutch enterprises) is very low; too much of Indonesia's wealth is drained off by smuggling. There is a great shortage of managerial skill and an Indonesian entrepreneur class—as distinct from the Chinese settled in Indonesia—has still to emerge. Salaries paid to the Indonesian civil servant have been made patently absurd by inflation. He often meets the situation by accepting bribes—in the form of cash or through the institution of receiving gifts which has been developed into a fine art—taking on extra jobs, hiring out his car, having his wife work and through numerous other ingenious means.

Conventional economics, however, are not always a reliable guide to an unconventional situation and it is only too easy to exaggerate Indonesia's difficulties. It is important to remember that about 70% of Indonesia's 97 million people are in the countryside and live off the land. To many of them inflation and food shortages mean that their produce fetches high prices. Tension in towns and cities, on the other hand, would seem to be growing. Obviously, Indonesia does not have unlimited time to set its economic house in order.

Indonesia is fabulously rich in resources. There is a saying that if you push a stick into the ground, it will sprout into a tree. The country is fertile and green and presents a striking contrast to the baked earth one sees on a train journey in India. Indonesian leaders are very conscious of their riches and they seem to believe that somehow things will be set right economically. There is little awareness yet that to develop riches in the context of modern power, ordered and efficient programmes and skills are necessary.

Talking to non-Government leaders of political parties in Djakarta in January, I came to the sad conclusion that they were engaged in only one level of activity—the political. The political parties have no concrete or practical programmes of bettering the economy. They take refuge behind resolutions and declarations. Even the Communist Party does not seem to have any immediate and practical method of bettering the country. Mr D.N. Aidit, the party's Chairman, told me that his party could play a very limited role in the economic field as long as it was not represented in the Cabinet—not the kind of answer one would expect from the main functionary of a powerful Communist Party.

Indonesia abandoned parliamentary democracy in 1959 and switched over to "Guided Democracy within the framework of the 1945 Constitution". Over the years President Soekarno has assumed wide powers; he is now both the President and the Prime Minister—the head of his team of Ministers is designated First Minister.

The President's mandate technically is from the People's Congress—a conglomeration of political parties, functional groups (including the Armed Forces) and regional representatives—which is required to meet at least once in five years. The President's team of Ministers is responsible only to him, the main function of Parliament being to process laws. The Supreme Advisory Council has a purely subsidiary role: it tenders advice to the President.

President Soekarno enjoys more power than he has had at any time. But while Bung Karno, as he is affectionately called by his people, is all powerful, he utilizes the various organs of the constitutional apparatus to feel the pulse of the country as also to keep the delicate balance of forces in check. While these bodies, therefore, do not possess power as they would in a parliamentary set-up, they are made to play a useful, though restricted, role. Parliament has twice returned Bills—the Press and Elections Bills—without approving them.

In turn, the ebullient politicians of Indonesia utilize the constitutional organs as a sounding board for their ideas and exert indirect pressure through them. At a recent meeting of the Supreme Advisory Council, for instance, Mr Aidit tried to push the NASAKOM idea, which in this case boiled down to Communist representation in the Cabinet. He did not succeed.

President Soekarno's main ideological objective has been to weld the different forces into one Indonesian outlook. This theme has been developed into the NASAKOM idea, which represents a projected fusion of nationalist, religious and Communist streams of thought. Two other pronounced tendencies—the Armed Forces' aspirations and regional prickliness—are accommodated through the role assigned to functional groups and by regional representation.

Politicians in Djakarta talk about the brief era of parliamentary democracy with sadness or contempt. "It was worse than France before de Gaulle", they say. Political parties, in fact, proliferated like mushroom and a predictable outcome of the downfall of parliamentary democracy was a desire to keep tight control over parties. This desire was accentuated by the Armed Forces' dislike of political parties, although they have learnt to take a mellower attitude today.

To be recognized as a legal party, a political organization must not only be countrywide in character with a minimum certified membership but must also subscribe to the national ideology of Panch Sheel. In practice, this has meant that the Communist Party will not make any propaganda against religion and the religious parties must not propagate the idea of a theocratic State. How sincere the PKI is in accepting the first principle of Panch Sheel (Belief in God) is another matter. Many non-Communist leaders suspect the Communists are paying lip service to the five objectives. Others argue that President Soekarno has succeeded in reducing the Communists to Titoist proportions.

In the spectrum of political parties, the PKI is in fact the only efficient and well organized party. Although it has not remained unaffected by the winds of change in the international Communist movement, it has fairly successfully confined its main energies to the internal situation. With a membership of over two million, it represents a powerful factor in the country.

Among the other parties, the PNI—the main nationalist party—is the largest, most amorphous and most widely split. It is at best problematic whether it can exercise a decisive influence over events; with President Soekarno in a commanding position, its role is very subsidiary. (Significantly, Dr Ali Sastroamidjojo, the PNI leader and twice a Prime Minister, has given his support to the NASAKOM idea—many PNI members do not agree with his views.)

The main recognized religious party, the Nahdatul Ulama, seems to have attracted a number of rather apolitical men. The strong Masjumi Party is outlawed—partly for its role in the last uprising—but still exercises influence through underground organizations and youth and other supposedly non-political groups.

The legitimacy of the Armed Forces' role in governing the country is taken for granted in Indonesia. Army leaders themselves refer to it as inevitable, in view of the background of the country's tempestuous independence struggle. The period of the emergency—the last of which was promulgated for the West Irian crisis—has naturally meant an acquisition of strength for the Army. Through chairmanship of committees in the provinces and other more direct means, the Army was for a time in an almost unassailable position.

During the last year, however, the Army's strength has been diluted, first by the diminution of General Nasution's position—he is now Chief of the Armed Forces while the President retains his position as Supreme Commander with each of the service chiefs directly under him as commanders. Next—and inevitably—the Communists successfully insisted on an end to the emergency now that the West Irian issue is settled. Again, the Armed Forces' Budget has been cut from about 75% to 47% of the General Budget. How effective this cut will be remains to be seen.

Although the Armed Forces have therefore been somewhat cut down to size, they remain a powerful factor in the country. Some of the seniormost Armed Forces officers I met impressed me by their shrewdness and capability. It was made plain to me that the Army had no intention whatsoever of relinquishing real power, even after the ending of the emergency on May 1. The Army has moreover successfully resisted demobilization proposals, and a part of the Army is now to be utilized in civil teams for development work. These teams will naturally be utilized for their political impact upon the people.

The political parties on the other hand seem to be much exercised over the position of Ministers in the Cabinet. At present the Ministers can keep afloat in the sea of Indonesian politics as long as they retain the President's confidence. Political parties as such cannot exercise any control over them although in selecting his Ministers, Bung Karno takes into account their political propensities. This the political parties find very irksome since it is a daily reminder of their lack of real power.

There is therefore much criticism of individual Ministers and the many ailments—and principally the economic difficulties—are blamed on them. Some parties hopefully look to the much postponed and still receding general elections to right the wrongs; according to one shrewd veteran politician, the general elections will not be held before the latter half of next year.

Although all parties speak in the context of Panch Sheel and Presidential decrees—I heard no talk of a return to parliamentary democracy—individual politicians behave as they would in a liberal set-up. Indeed, if one were to take for granted the restrictions under which political parties function, there is little to distinguish them from parties elsewhere.

One achievement the political parties have to their credit is that they have—for the present—successfully scuttled the original idea of the National Front which was conceived as something of a Government party and the principal channel of communication between the President and the people. Political parties are in fact members of the National Front; the role of this organization however, apart from the benefits the Communist Party is deriving from it, is rather subsidiary. Also, the unanimity and fire the political parties displayed in opposing the Elections Bill, which would have further reduced their powers, last year were an interesting indication of their feelings.

In this picture of Indonesia, two main political forces have emerged as the main contenders for power—the Communist Party and the Armed Forces, the latter broadly representing an anti-Communist force. The present is a relatively stable phase in Indonesian politics because each side recognizes its weaknesses and will not easily give an opportunity to the other to capitalize on its mistakes. The abortive Madiun revolt, for instance, was a serious mistake of the Communists. The Army, on the other hand, is more conscious of its limitations in carrying the country with it.

Given this situation, President Soekarno has merely to distribute power equally between the Army and the PKI to neutralize both, leaving for himself a wide area of activity. Effective power is therefore largely concentrated in Bung Karno's hands and, to some extent, lies with those closely associated with him. How far the President's close advisers give him an opportunity to know the facts about his country is a matter of much speculation in Djakarta. This is, indeed, an old problem familiar to the world; it is merely being enacted in a new setting.

Much of Indonesian politics revolves round personalities. The President is a "young man of 60", as one of his Ministers says. He is dynamic and is essentially the unifier. Temperamentally, he is recognized as an artist as well as an engineer—he is in fact a graduate of Bandung's Technical College.

General Nasution is a Sumatran, a good Muslim and a respected soldier. He is, besides, an upright man. The General's mistake politically has been that he took too much for granted, particularly about the Army's political and other capabilities. The Armed Forces have also been "tainted by power", a phrase used to refer to the partial responsibility the Army must share for the economic difficulties, and for the corruption prevalent in Army ranks—the General himself is above reproach in this matter.

Mr D.N. Aidit has successfully retained his position as Chairman and leader of the PKI. At times he gives in to the dominant pro-Peking wing, but prefers to take a non-committal line on the prickly issues of international Communism. Mr Aidit is an astute and likeable man who has developed to a remarkable extent the image of the Indonesian nationalist Communist.

Dr Hatta, that respected figure of Indonesian constitutionalism, leads an elegant retired life in Djakarta. There is still an occasional mention of his name in political circles, but he gives very much the impression of being a back-number in Indonesia's fast moving political world. Whether a later situation will bring him back to power is a very problematic question.

There are on the Indonesian firmament other personalities, ready and anxious to make a spectacular entry on the political stage. Only time can tell which of them will achieve national status and power.

The Communists, on present showing, are prepared to bide their time. Optimistic assessments of their present strength in the country are around 25%. The Army has learnt to be patient. There is, however, some talk of the Army combining with Masjumi elements to achieve power "after Bung Karno". Some Nationalist politicians on the other hand hope—somewhat wistfully—that the Army will rule the country with them. The future is for the crystal gazer.

9

Opposition members of Parliament talk about buying and selling Jaguars in the lounge of the PWD office that serves as the temporary home of Malaya's Parliament in Kuala Lumpur. Mr Aziz bin Ishak, the former Agriculture Minister and now a contestant for the prickly crown of Leader of the Opposition, flits from one table to another with a studious air of absentmindedness, a plume of orchid in his buttonhole. He holds a pipe and tin of tobacco in one hand, bulging briefcase in the other.

In the Chamber, a sardonic smile settles on Mr Tan Siew Sin, the Finance Minister. The eloquence of the Opposition Pan-Malayan Islamic Party leaders could well be a brook of clear running water safely siphoned to the sea, as far as Mr Tan is concerned.

In the Malayan House of Representatives, the Opposition controls about 30 of the 104 seats. The different and contradictory elements that go to make the Opposition got together in March to agree, for the first time, to a joint statement condemning the Alliance Government's method of dealing with the Malaysia concept. Mr Aziz was chairman of a committee that hammered out this statement.

The PMIP, which controls the biggest block of Opposition seats, is most earnest in debating Malaysia. This party is an alloy of religious extremism and nationalism and stands for a coming together of the Malay race from Southern Thailand to the Philippines. A bitter quarrel with Indonesia therefore goes against its grain. The PMIP took steps to ban Western ballroom dancing in Kelantan State on the ground that it was demoralizing, but is apparently having second thoughts on the practical implications of this policy.

The Socialist Front is bereft of its leader, Mr Ahmad Boestamam, who was detained by the Government in February on charges of subversion and alleged connexions with the Indonesian Communists. His arrest provided the Opposition with much ammunition in Parliament's last session, which it did not always use to best advantage.

Mr Boestamam is leader of Malaya's Malay-based Rakyat Party; the other constituent of the Front is the Chinese-based Labour Party whose leader, Mr Lim Kean Siew, a lawyer, continues to lend zest to the Opposition. The Socialist Front has yet to capture power in a State. Meanwhile, it makes best use of its stronghold, the Penang island, to put an attractive Socialist gloss on local Government. It runs the City Council.

The People's Progressive Party is content to fortify its urban strongholds in Perak State in the predominantly Chinese areas. The public front of the PPP is presented by the two Seenivasagam brothers, both of them successful lawyers, who are in the forefront in attacking Malay privileges—for the benefit of a largely Chinese clientele.

The rather new United Democratic Party is another Chinese-based party, even more extreme in orientation than the PPP. For such diverse elements to come together to condemn Tengku Abdul Rahman's handling of the Malaysia concept required a rather unusual catalytic agent. This was provided by the mass arrests of politicians in Malaya and Singapore in February and the fear that the Government would do what it liked with a divided Opposition. The elections of 1964 are also beginning to cast their shadow; now is the time to work for electoral understandings to prevent the splintering of votes.

In this chequerboard of political parties and the racial overtones that necessarily go with party politics in Malaya, the crisis in Malayan-Indonesian relations has created new stresses and strains. About 60% of Malays, who are the dominant political factor in Malaya, are said to be of Indonesian stock. Although many associations representing Malays of Indonesian stock have dutifully condemned Indonesia's confrontation policy, the problem remains acute.

The ruling Alliance Government has reacted to the crisis by linking Indonesia's confrontation with the machinations of the Indonesian Communist Party. The official line propagated by Kuala Lumpur is that the Indonesian people are being misled by the allegedly dominant PKI.

On the other hand, UMNO has successfully employed the racial texture of the country to win added support from the Chinese. Significantly, it was Mr Tan Siew Sin who rather discreetly employed an argument privately used by the Indonesians in opposing Malaysia (that it would lead to greater Chinese influence) to win the support of the local Chinese against Indonesia's confrontation policy. UMNO seems to have lost some support among Malays.

For the Opposition parties, this situation has led to renewed efforts to look for a Malay leader as an alternative to the indisputably popular Tengku Abdul Rahman. Mr. Aziz filled the role of chairman of the committee that drafted the Opposition statement on Malaysia because he is at the moment partyless, having been expelled by the United Malays National Organization. But there are formidable hurdles to his assuming the role of the leader of a joint Opposition.

PMIP leaders believe that this honour should go to one of them since they control the largest block of seats in the Opposition. Some other Opposition leaders have doubts about Mr Aziz's potentialities to win support against the Tengku. His personal following among sections of UMNO seems to be contracting. He has waited too long to organize his own political party out of his support in the co-operatives.

Mr Aziz told me he enjoyed the support of half of the nation's co-operative members, i.e. of 200,000.

Mr Aziz plans to assess his actual strength in the co-operatives before launching a new party. In March, he talked to me about various other fields in which the Opposition could follow an agreed common policy—in propagating a non-aligned policy for Malaya in world affairs, in pleading for co-operatives to market produce in the country. Prickly questions like the language issue would be left severely alone.

According to the PPP leader, Mr D.R. Seenivasagam, Opposition parties are closer to each other than ever before since 1958. This is true, but even so Opposition unity can at best be momentary and limited. The constituents of the Alliance Government being in power can take a reasonably moderate view of conflicting racial interests. Opposition parties often have to take more extreme attitudes to gather support (it is significant that even the legal party of the Left, the Socialist Front, is composed of two parties, one Malay-based and the other Chinese-oriented). Opposition parties are against the present concept of Malaysia for their own and differing reasons. Divisive forces within the Opposition are many although electoral arrangements at the regional, if not the national, level will be made—at the expense of the Alliance Government.

The United Malays National Organization and its two associates, however, need have no serious worries as far as the next elections are concerned. Political democracy is still in a rather rudimentary stage in Malaya and it is difficult to take some Opposition leaders seriously. The prosperous bulge in Malaya is also a serious factor in limiting opposition. Most Opposition leaders, for instance, drive to Parliament in sleek cars which they own.

The significance of recent events lies in the fact that the winds of change are gradually overtaking Malaya. Only a few months ago, political extremism in Malaya was aligned almost exclusively with sections of the Chinese population, the Malays providing the solid rock of a somnolent political stability. Indonesia's confrontation policy has shown that Malays can also prove combustible.

Some Opposition leaders openly talk of difficult times and disturbances ahead. Others, including Dr Burhanuddin of the PMIP, say that independence was handed to Malaya on a platter and that Tengku Abdul Rahman is not a genuine leader of the Malays because he was formerly a civil servant of the British Malayan Government. To disprove his critics, the Tengku has to demonstrate that he can effectively lead his people in times of grave crisis as in times of peace.

10

There comes a time in the life of a nation when the old order changes, yielding place to new. In the Philippines, this phenomenon has synchronized with the accession to Presidency of Mr Diasdado Macapagal.

Filipinos try to interpret this change in various ways. President Macapagal himself explained it to me in the context of his country's relations with the USA. The son is now grown up, he said, and while he continues to have deep regard for his foster parents, he is striking an independent course.

The Vice-President and Foreign Secretary, Mr Pelaez, described the new stirrings as part of a process of growing up. "You from India", he said half in jest, "were responsible for egging us on. At international conferences you used to tell us we were American stooges".

The ordinary Filipino, on the other hand, is somewhat bewildered by the winds of change. A jazz performer asked me in all earnestness: "Do you think we should be Asians?"

The Spaniards were among the earliest European colonizers in Asia, and after more than three centuries of Spanish rule in the Philippines came the Americans. The American presence in the capacity of rulers lasted less than 50 years; it was just sufficient to give a veneer of American life and habits to a people predominantly influenced by Spain and Catholicism.

Years after the people of the Philippines achieved the status of an independent nation, they continued to regard themselves as European in outlook. Being an overwhelmingly Catholic nation set them apart from their neighbours, and the attractive blend long years of Spanish association has produced in the indigenous inhabitants induced in them a taste for occidental ways of life.

It was, however, inevitable that the years after Bandung should have had an effect on the Philippines. The first conscious effort to follow an Asian policy in world affairs was made during the Nacionalista Administration—now in the Opposition. But it needed a man of the calibre of President Macapagal and the claim to North Borneo to launch the Philippines truly on the new path.

President Macapagal would not have officially espoused the claim to North Borneo in the first year of his Administration if it were not for Malaysia's impending formation. Malaysia thus served as a catalytic agent for the claim, but the President's interest in it has been long and assiduous. As a Congressman, he introduced a resolution on the claim in the Congress; as a lawyer, he is convinced of its strength; as a politician, of its potentialities.

The Philippine Press played its part in getting the claim launched. A vociferous campaign was set into motion from the time of Mr Macapagal's accession to Presidency at the end of 1961, which culminated in the Congress adopting a unanimous resolution supporting the claim. The President's official espousal of the claim was not immediate; he gave the impression of stalling.

The claim was too much of a gift to give away to the Opposition at home. The President was naturally conscious of the substantial Muslim minority in Southern Philippines and the effect coldshouldering the claim would have on them. There were the other obvious repercussions to think of: the effect it would have on the then friendly relations with Malaya and on the Association of South-East Asia, its effect on the Philippine commitments with the USA and Britain and how it would affect Communism in South-East Asia.

The President did not stake the claim without deliberation although he could hardly have been aware of all the repercussions it has had. At first the claim was made in somewhat general terms and hesitantly but the British reaction—in effect, telling the Philippines to keep their hands off Malaysia—set the seal on it. The British have had to pay dearly for misreading the mind and temper of President Macapagal, and they have since been busy retracing their steps from the original position of not countenancing the claim.

The British were not alone in misreading the situation. Against the past background of the Philippines, the claim sounded ridiculous. How could the Philippines go against the Malaysia project which was designed to contain the threat of Communism in South-East Asia? it was asked. The Philippines, it was assumed, would bend before American pressure.

Partly, the Philippine authorities themselves were responsible for the distorted picture of the claim the outside world received. There was an insufficient attempt to explain their case, until in December the Brunei revolt raised larger issues of Malaysia's validity. The Philippines, so to speak, jumped on the bandwagon of Malaysia's opponents and grasped the opportunity of letting Mr Azahari sojourn in Manila during the most sensitive period of the Brunei revolt.

In this attitude of defiance, the Philippines inevitably came closer to Indonesia. It was not so much a case of Indonesia leading Manila up the garden path—as is sometimes made out—but of the two sides recognizing their interests in cultivating friendlier relations. While Indonesia is naturally anxious to fight its battle against Malaysia in unison with Manila, the latter is equally anxious to further its new image of independence by forging closer links with Djakarta.

In a sense, the Philippines would not have gone as far as they have in asserting their new independence in thought if it were not for events. Sometimes, this results in the impression that Filipino arguments opposing Malaysia are an afterthought. However, many Filipino leaders have convinced themselves (whatever the reasons that led them to be so convinced) that Malaysia is evil, and that far from containing Communism, it will promote subversion.

Filipino arguments are very interesting, if not entirely convincing. To begin with, Filipinos regard Singapore with horror; to them it is the hotbed of Communism and Chinese extremism. Since they do not believe there can be any permanence about restrictions of entry from Singapore into the Borneo territories once Malaysia is formed, they think the new Federation will merely provide Communism with a ladder to climb into North Borneo, which is 18 miles from the Philippines at its closest point.

On the other hand, run the Filipino arguments, the island States can band together (Malaya being an archipelago is included) against the threat of Chinese Communism. This argument presupposes that sooner or later the mainland areas of South-East Asia will fall under Chinese influence—not a very optimistic assessment of the people's capacity to withstand Communism.

The importance of these arguments is not that they are valid but that they are being seriously propagated. How far the Indonesians have influenced Filipinos must remain a matter of speculation although there has been an extensive exchange of ideas between leaders of the two countries and the Filipinos have been in a receptive mood. However, only in respect of one argument expressed by some of the Filipino leaders—that the "Tengku is a British stooge"—did I get the distinct feeling that their ideas were borrowed.

The claim itself has now been left behind by events. Its legal aspects need not detain us here (the Filipino case is not as weak as is made out to be). Malaya is now willing to have it referred to the World Court after Malaysia is formed and this would ultimately satisfy the Philippines.

The most interesting development is the finesse with which President Macapagal is championing the idea of a summit conference of the Philippines, Malaya and Indonesia. The President has already scored a minor victory by persuading Tengku Abdul Rahman to support the summit idea in principle. He must have dispelled some of the fears of the Tengku as far as the objects of the proposed conference are concerned. Getting the Tengku and President Soekarno to face each other across a conference table is a much more difficult task, but the new role of mediator President Macapagal is playing has intriguing possibilities and indirectly the inference that the Philippines and Indonesia have not quite "ganged up" against Malaya, as the Tengku fears.

So far President Macapagal has succeeded in projecting the Philippines on the world stage (in the earlier stages, not to the country's advantage). The Opposition does not publicly question the new direction of his foreign policy; it cannot afford to. But even in his own Liberal Party there are differences of opinion on how far the Philippines should go in opposing Malaysia and a noticeable nervousness about the newly-formed friendship with Indonesia. On the Opposition side, one Senator has come out strongly in opposition to the claim. Characteristically, the President largely nullified his opposition by insinuating that the Senator was not entirely patriotic.

All Filipino leaders emphasize that theirs being a democratic country, they will press their claim only through constitutional means. But I found an under-current of feeling in Manila in April that somehow the Indonesians will act to prevent the formation of Malaysia.

This is only the beginning of the new direction Philippine foreign policy is taking. How far the country will go in asserting its mood of independence depends upon President Macapagal and events. An astute Senator of the Liberal Party told me that the Philippines will go as far as they can without straining Filipino-American relations to the breaking point. There are obvious limits set by the American military presence in the Philippines (stemming from the defence treaty) and the fact that Filipinos cannot defend themselves without American support. Philippine association with SEATO is less of an inhibiting factor.

The American pattern of Government adopted by the Philippines vests more power in the President than a Prime Minister enjoys in a parliamentary democracy. And President Macapagal is certainly a man to contend with—there are already Opposition cries of the President's alleged dictatorial approach.

Mr Macapagal is well schooled in the game of political in-fighting and the flair with which he announces new programmes speaks of his ability and ambitions. At the same time he is adopting an almost messianic approach to projecting his country on the world stage. A plus factor is his shrewd grasp of what is happening around him. The Philippine claim to North Borneo has thus become a symbol of a new forward-looking foreign policy.

11

There was a time not so long ago when the Malaysia project was being envisaged with high hopes. In Kuala Lumpur, the atmosphere was one of exuberance, with the Malayan Prime Minister setting the tone for a Happy Malaysia.

Kuala Lumpur was not unmindful of the opposition to Malaysia from the British Borneo territories of Sarawak and North Borneo. Much time and effort was spent in propagating the right image of the new Federation in the two Borneo territories and local chiefs and chieftains were invited to Malaya in a never-ending procession—for brainwashing, the Opposition wisecracked.

There was, of course, *the* problem of Singapore, but for which Malaysia would never have been launched. Essentially, this was a problem of containing the Chinese and the political extremism that went with them. The Borneo territories provided (supposedly) the much needed counterweight to Singapore, an island Malaya would not have been happy to lose. The immediate problem of getting Singapore to agree to Malaysia on the basis of a depressed vote for the island was left in the hands of Mr Lee Kuan Yew, who staged a so-called referendum to claim victory.

In North Borneo, Mr Donald Stephens proved the saviour. With great political skill, he swung the majority of the political parties towards Malaysia. Sarawak, with its rather large Chinese population, proved more difficult to win over or subdue, but Britain and Malaya did the next best thing—they isolated the Sarawak United People's Party as a distinctly Chinese organization.

And then Brunei hit the world headlines. For Malaya this was the unkindest cut of all because subversion, when it came, came from their brother Malays—not the Chinese, as was feared. Malaya in fact had been ignoring the tiny British Sultanate because it was felt there was no danger from that source. An all-powerful Malay Sultan was at the head of the Government and the ruling aristocracy was Malay. Mr Azahari could not really go against his Sultan. He did.

The catch phrase Happy Malaysia has now acquired an ironic ring. The impending Federation has brought to the surface the conflicting interests of political parties and neighbouring countries immersing South-East Asia in another crisis. The animosities and jealousies prevailing in the area have only served to harden the opposition and vastly complicate the picture.

As a scheme for decolonization, Malaysia was a good idea. The two British colonies of Sarawak and North Borneo and the tiny protectorate of Brunei are on the northern fringes of the Borneo island, the greater part of which is a unit of Indonesia. Since independence for the three territories would have meant an ultimate subsidiary relationship with Indonesia, the British were anxious to reduce the Borneo territories' vulnerability. By proposing Malaysia (the original idea was British, perhaps Mr Malcolm MacDonald's), they solved two problems at one stroke. They made the incorporation of the Borneo territories an attractive proposition for the Tengku since it would take care of Singapore's

Chineseness and they assured for themselves a continuing friendly relationship with the Borneo territories where they have substantial economic interests.

Self-interest does not necessarily make a good project bad but it lends teeth to Opposition cries of neocolonialism. Behind Indonesian opposition to Malaysia are a host of jealousies and fears, the most important of them—seldom expressed frankly—is the apprehension that Malaysia might encourage the latent centrifugal tendencies by leading to cession of the adjacent islands. Against the Indonesian background of revolts and the part played by Malayans in the Sumatra rebellion of 1958, this fear is not entirely a figment of the imagination.

The incompatibility of personalities (the Tengku on one hand and President Soekarno and Dr Subandrio on the other) has also served to harden Indonesian opposition to Malaysia. There is also the intriguing suggestion in this conflict of a rivalry for leadership. There is, besides, the background of a love-hate relationship between the two countries in which the desire for utilizing a common racial stock and religion to bring greater understanding alternates with the animosities brought about by differing levels of prosperity and the different ideological and political roads the two countries have chosen.

The Brunei revolt gave Indonesia the opportunity to express its suspicion of Malaysia and as abuses between Djakarta and Kuala Lumpur began piling up, Indonesian opposition took the form of confrontation in January. Confrontation is a handy Indonesian concept which can mean everything or nothing. In any case, Indonesia spelled out its opposition to Malaysia: it was neocolonial, it could subvert Indonesia and it was being imposed by a colonial Power against the wishes of the territories concerned.

Indonesia found a useful ally in the Philippines whose claim to North Borneo got mixed up with a Filipino desire to assert their independence of the USA and the West. Filipino opposition to Malaysia increased in inverse proportion to the scant respect their claim to North Borneo received in the world, and an initial British refusal even to talk about the claim only intensified Manila's desire to prosecute it. The Brunei revolt also provided the Philippines with an opportunity to demonstrate their dislike of Malaysia by playing host to Mr Azahari during the first weeks of the revolt.

Indonesian propaganda on the Malaysia issue is strikingly similar to that used in its earlier claim to West Irian. There were protest marches, demonstrations, resolutions and solidarity meetings in Djakarta. The elastic confrontation policy was itself modelled on Djakarta's action in relation to the Dutch. But whereas in the latter case Indonesia had the moral support of most Asian countries, in the former only the Communists came out on their side. It was perhaps because of this lack of general support that Indonesia for a time mellowed its confrontation policy and that no battalions of volunteers ventured into the Borneo territories from Indonesia.

In another respect, however, Indonesia has been remarkably successful. It has been able to project to a large part of the Asian world that the Malaysia project, being British in origin, is being pushed through by them with the Tengku being used merely as their instrument. In view of Malaya's pro-West orientation and the 30-year defence treaty it has with Britain, the Indonesian image of the Tengku has been accepted in some very unlikely places.

Malaysia's best selling point was the containment of Chinese Communism it set out to offer. There is no country in the region which is not anxious to stem either the Chinese or Communism or both.

Indonesia's initial attitude to Malaysia was proper and it was, ironically enough, the Malayan Prime Minister who offered Djakarta the excuse to take a different posture. Tengku Abdul Rahman, in a speech to a political rally, asked Indonesia to "keep its hands off Malaysia" on the strength of what Dr Ali Sastroamidjojo had said.

Malayan proneness to making retorts merely intensified and brought to a head Indonesian suspicions of Malaysia; they did not create them. And having decided to take a diplomatic offensive against Malaysia, Indonesia set about countering the most effective arguments for the new Federation.

Indonesia set out to prove—in behind-the-scene briefings in world capitals—that Malaysia would promote Chinese influence, rather than stem it. Its main argument rested on the presumption that by making the British Borneo territories political units of a Federation which would also comprise Singapore and Malaya, Malaysia would open the door to an unrestricted flow of Chinese subversive elements from Singapore. These elements, it was suggested, could easily infiltrate into Indonesian Borneo and the Philippines.

Indonesians presented these arguments in the context of increased difficulties they would have in containing the three million Chinese who were already posing a problem for them. And for the benefit of anti-Communist nations such as the Philippines, Indonesians linked the issue with the delicate balance of power maintained by President Soekarno at home.

Singapore's radicalism and overwhelming Chinese population have long symbolized a most undesirable combination for many countries in the region. It was therefore easy to paint the turbulent island as one radiating subversion to the islands of Indonesia and the Philippines. This argument was understandable to these countries also in terms of the smuggling which goes on between the Borneo territories and Indonesia and the Philippines.

It would be fair to say that only Indonesia and the Philippines subscribed to the line of thinking first propagated by Djakarta. But the Brunei revolt again came to Indonesia's rescue, weakening Malaysia's merit by casting doubts on its internal strength. Less than 20,000 Brunei Malays were directly or indirectly involved in the December revolt. But its significance was to dramatize to a world audience the opposition of a proposed constituent unit of Malaysia.

And the chain reaction the revolt had in Malaya, Singapore and the other two Borneo territories again brought to the surface the opposition to Malaysia in these territories. Not all of this opposition was—or is—Communist. This was recently illustrated by all Opposition parties in Malaya getting together to condemn Tengku Abdul Rahman's method of handling the Malaysia concept. Nobody quarrels with Malaysia as a concept but each party and country has its own concept.

Nor is the presence of a large number of British troops in the Borneo territories and the introduction of fresh troops into Sarawak a good advertisement for Malaysia. Nearly five months after the Brunei revolt, stragglers are still keeping troops busy. In Sarawak, disturbances are feared and all non-native inhabitants have been asked to hand in their arms in parts of the territory. This measure, it was officially stated, was aimed at the Chinese because Communists (according to the Government spokesman, all of them are Chinese) had set out to subvert Malaysia through violence. North Borneo is relatively quiet.

In Singapore, the Government has had to make mass arrests of some 120 politicians, trade unionists and students. In Malaya, the number of those arrested under the preventive detention law was at one stage around 60.

From these facts Indonesians and other opponents of Malaysia argue that the new Federation cannot be a stabilizing factor since, far from promoting stability, it has already caused a crisis. The classic answer to this is, of course, that much of the crisis has been caused by Indonesia's own attitude towards Malaysia, not its impending formation.

There is, however, no gainsaying the fact that because of the composition of Malaysia and the opposition this has produced, besides the attitudes adopted by the two neighbouring countries, the new Federation is a much less attractive proposition than it was assumed to be. It is obviously too late in the day for Britain or Malaya to retrace their steps—assuming that either of them would want to. One of the objectives of Indonesia's confrontation policy was apparently to make the Tengku have second thoughts on Malaysia. In any event, the consequences of calling a halt to Malaysia would perhaps be graver than from proceeding with it.

Malaya's trump card is that no one has offered any practical alternative. President Macapagal's conception of a confederation—to include Malaya with Indonesia and the Philippines—still remains a concept and is full of prickly implications once one gets down to details. Malaya has, in fact, privately told Manila that the formation of Malaysia would not preclude the confederation from taking shape at a later date.

The other suggestion—proposed by a number of Opposition parties in Malaya and the Borneo territories—is that the three Borneo territories should be given independence first by themselves. This solution is not as simple as it sounds since Mr Azahari's concept of Brunei ruling the other two territories would not prove acceptable to the latter, and the British objection to it would be that the arrangement would unfairly expose the territories to Indonesian influence.

12

Nearly six years after independence, some of Malaya's nine traditional rulers are getting restive and are protesting against the straitjacket the Federal Constitution has put them in.

The Sultan of Selangor called a Press conference in May, thumped a table and asked why he should be discriminated against, instead of being accorded special privileges, in the purchase of choice land in Kuala Lumpur. Before him the Sultan of Perak blamed the Alliance Government in the State for neglecting its duties. This provoked Tengku Abdul Rahman (himself a prince by birth and related by marriage to some of the Sultans) to issue a stern warning about the way kings and princes had gone in India and other parts of the world.

The crisis has been papered over. The Conference of Rulers—the princes' club provided by the Federal Constitution—has met and acquiesced in passing a vote of confidence in the Government, after, it is reported, a deathly silence of 10 minutes.

Yet this is only the beginning—not the end—of a historical conflict between the princes and popular leaders of Malaya. In the dust raised by the outbursts of the two rulers, the air is already thick with prophecies that the days of the Sultans are numbered. While Malaya's princes might eventually go the way of many kings, this conflict—when it acquires more serious proportions—is bound to take an interesting turn. The dice is not loaded entirely against the Sultans.

Immediately after Malaya's independence, the Sultans served a very useful political purpose. They became the rallying point for Malay, as opposed to Chinese-or Indian-oriented, nationalism. The Malayan Union Constitution was scrapped and the present Federal Constitution, giving Malays special position and privileges, brought in.

In this scheme of things it was natural that the Sultans should be accorded a special position. They became constitutional monarchs in their States and Malay privileges were hung on them. Each of the Sultans (a few call themselves differently) has become the particular protector of Malay interests and of Islam. While he is bound to accept the advice of his executive council—unlike in former days—no law directly affecting his privileges and position can be passed without the consent of the Conference of Rulers.

It thus comes about that in a country the size of Greece (51,000 square miles) there are nine monarchs, each maintaining extensive establishments, each distributing honours and titles, each celebrating his birthday with fanfare, each having his own subjects, each a king in his own realm.

This arrangement directly costs the Malayan taxpayer something of the order of M$ 10 million a year. Personal allowances of the Sultans vary. The Sultan of Johore gets a personal tax-free allowance of M$ 20,000 a month; the Raja of Perlis M$ 5,000 a month; the Sultan of Perak M$ 14,000 per month. Each of their consorts also receives a personal allowance and so do the rulers' close kinsmen.

These allowances—and others for the maintenance of their establishments—are paid by the respective States. The Yang di-Pertuan Agong (literally He who is made Great Lord), Malaya's Paramount Ruler and constitutional head elected once every five years by the nine Sultans from among themselves in order of seniority, is paid by the Federal Government. His personal allowance tax-free is M$ 15,000 a month and his consort's M$ 2,500 a month.

Apart from these moneys directly paid to the Sultans and their kinsmen and the allotments for their establishments, they enjoy valuable privileges. Their vehicles do not pay road tax, they cannot be proceeded against in a court of law, they receive the benefits of duty-free imports.

Judged by Indian standards, the Sultans are not rich. Only one of them, the 69-year-old Sultan of Johore, belongs to the millionaire class. There are two reasons for this. The Muslim law of inheritance has, over the years, fragmented wealth and property and in some States, notably in Perak and Negri Sembilan, the rulers are elected from among a number of royal families instead of automatically inheriting their thrones.

The interests of the Sultans vary. The present Paramount Ruler, whose substantive position is that of the Raja of Perlis, cultivates orchids and plays golf. The Sultan of Trengganu, the present Deputy Paramount Ruler, is a good photographer. The Sultan of Johore is a keen hunter. The Sultan of Perak paints and designs boats. The Sultan of Pahang, who was twice passed over by the Conference of Rulers apparently for contracting controversial marriages, is a good polo player (handicap plus 4) and keeps a string of polo ponies.

Some Sultans also play host to visiting beauty queens. Many have undertaken extensive travels and many went to the Malay College in Kuala Kangsar in north-west Malaya, which occupied a position somewhat similar to that of the Chiefs' College in Lahore.

It is significant that the two Sultans who raised a public controversy over their status are among the five rulers belonging to the younger set who ascended their thrones after independence. Politicians in Kuala Lumpur say that they feel frustrated because they do not enjoy real power and still have some archaic notions about the divine right of kings. There is no doubt that some of the younger rulers have begun to tire of the trappings of power without its contents.

This feeling will obviously prove to be a source of conflict in the future, particularly when a growing Malay elite is having second thoughts on the value of the institution as against the costs incurred.

The Sultans' strong point is in the symbolic value they represent in protecting Malay, as opposed to non-Malay, rights and privileges. In a country in which the peculiar amalgam of races impinges on every activity, the Sultans are heads of intricately built edifices to ensure that the Malays remain politically dominant and, in future, become economically so. Any tampering with the top of the edifice can have serious repercussions.

Malay politicians, including Tengku Abdul Rahman, are therefore wary about approaching the issue. Angry Sultans would be too valuable a gift to give to the Opposition. Malaya's Sultans have many more years of privilege to look forward to, unless another storm brings them into the centre of controversy.

13

Manila is beginning to acquire some of the magic conjured by Bandung in South-East Asia. Even as preparations are being made in July for the three-nation summit conference among Indonesia, Malaya and the Philippines, Manila has come to represent a new phase in the turbulent politics of the region.

This phase is variously described by various people. To Indonesians must go the credit of coining the catchiest slogans, and Indonesia has decided on the word Maphilindo for the getting together of the three nations. Filipinos are the keenest and most enthusiastic about the desire of the peoples of Malay race to club together. It was, in fact, the elegant Vice-President of the Philippines, Mr Emmanuel Pelaez, who first spoke about a summit conference to sort out mutual suspicions and animosities between Malaya and Indonesia. Thailand, at first included in the proposal, has been left out.

Malaya's response to the Greater Malaysia Confederation, although correct, is complicated by the diversity of its peoples. The political and ideological driving force of this project can only be a desire to emphasize the Malayness of the peoples of the three countries and, specifically, to contain the danger of Chinese expansionism.

Welcome though this idea is to the Malays of Malaya (even Government leaders of the United Malays National Organization take every opportunity to decry the wealth of the Malayan Chinese), they cannot profess to be too enthusiastic about it.

The June Foreign Ministers' conference in Manila decided that the heads of the three Governments should meet once a year and so should their Foreign Ministers. Also, the three countries should set up national secretariats for the purpose, pending the eventual formation of a joint secretariat.

The confederation idea has been accepted only in principle and what is ultimately envisaged is a regional commonwealth of nations. The Manila conference documents specifically preclude the handing over of sovereignty by any of the nations, and Tengku Abdul Rahman was at pains to tell me in Kuala Lumpur during an interview that the systems of Government of the three countries were too diverse to permit anything more than close co-operation among the three.

In Manila, much time was spent by the Foreign Ministers in hammering out the agreed statements. There was at one point discussion on the relative merits of rival dictionaries and hours were spent on deciding the appropriateness of particular phrases. One session lasted till three in the morning. The concessions which made these agreements possible were debated in private (Filipino delegates were particularly impressed by the debating skill of Malaya's Permanent Secretary in the Foreign Office in Kuala Lumpur, Mr Ghazali bin Shafie).

The newly-found brotherly spirit in Manila has diverse causes. For Indonesia, the realization of her economic troubles coupled with the need for Western aid, the anti-Chinese riots in Java and the outer islands and the failure of her propaganda effort combined to induce a mood of reason.

For the Philippines, the transition was easier. The claim to North Borneo brought the Philippines on the world stage. President Macapagal grasped the opportunity to project himself and his country as more independent entities. But with time it became apparent that the President was more interested in bringing the summit to fruition than to go on pursuing a rather futile claim.

Malaya, sick with worry over Malaysia's implications because of Indonesia's hostility, was only too happy to clutch at any peace offer. The first moves to what eventually led to the Tengku-Soekarno meeting in Tokyo at the end of May were made by Indonesia several months before. But Malaya was tortured by her doubts about Indonesia's sincerity and vitriolic prose continued to flow out of Djakarta for some time.

Filipinos now talk about the confederation with much romanticism. They speak about developing the vast wilds of North Borneo with Malay, as opposed to Chinese, labour; of the limitless possibilities of building up complementary trade (Indonesia to concentrate on oil, Malaya on rubber and tin and the Philippines on copra); in short, of doing business with each other without "outside interference".

This phrase has acquired a symbolic significance for the Filipinos. Out of their desire to come closer to Asia and to display a new mood of independence, they are the most zealous in demanding that the three nations settle their problems by themselves. The Filipinos noted, for instance, the "British reserve" of Tun Abdul Razak at social gatherings in Manila in June. Indonesian camaraderie, on the other hand, particularly impressed them. The Indonesians also paid their hosts a compliment by donning the embroidered Manila bush-shirt.

To the Indonesians, the confederation idea is almost equally, though not as romantically, welcome. Manila was a particular concession they made for their national interest but the idea of a Greater Indonesia, as it was at one time conceived by Indonesian leaders, holds a fascination for many of them. And the anti-Chinese riots in Java only intensified Indonesian interest in the confederation.

Even the dichotomy in Malayan thinking cannot hide Malays' thrill in envisaging a union of the Malay race stretching grandiosely across South-East Asia. A union of 140 million people, say the Malay advocates.

To what heights of practical co-operation the confederation will take the three countries it is still too early to say. However, Manila has already reversed the trend towards conflagration in the area and has implanted in the minds of millions of people the romance implied by the prospect of a getting together of the Malay race.

This by itself is a substantial achievement for the Philippines, particularly President Macapagal, who was doubtless helped by circumstances. And the new emphasis being laid on the right of the three countries to maintain their national identities as also their primary responsibility for the region's security, in spite of the Philippine dependence on the USA and Malaya's on Britain, is an indication of the way the wind is blowing.

It will not be all smooth sailing for Maphilindo in the future—national moods and policies can change—but Manila has set in motion a new spirit and a new idea. The summit conference at the end of July will crown this achievement with toasts of champagne.

14

Singapore's taps did not run dry one Saturday in July. The daily 12-hour water rationing on the island, enforced because of a drought, was lifted for a day because Mr Lee Kuan Yew was returning from London after signing the Malaysia agreement with Malaya, Sabah (North Borneo) and Sarawak—Brunei decided to remain out of Malaysia because of its Sultan's desire to play for independence.

Radio Singapore had been preparing the people for the Prime Minister's return. He was to receive a hero's welcome; even the number of people who would be at the airport had been prophesied—20,000. Flags and bunting and banners were fluttering in the city. The route of the Prime Minister's entry was chalked out and the procession was to end its journey on the steps of the City Hall where the traditional lion dancers would regale the crowds.

All of this did happen on the Saturday, and more. Within the space of four hours Mr Lee made six speeches—three at the airport, one each in Malay, English and the Hokkien dialect, and he repeated the exercise on the steps of the City Hall. It was a triumphant Lee who spoke at the airport. He told his audience with much delight of how he had outmanoeuvred the British Commonwealth Secretary, Mr Duncan Sandys, of how he got the better of the Malayan

Finance Minister, Mr Tan Siew Sin, of how he "sacrificed" M$ 5 million as a gesture of goodwill to Tengku Abdul Rahman, of how stupid Singapore's Opposition parties were.

The theme of his speeches in the city was the same but Mr Lee was less exultant and fell more often to repeating cliches about Malaysia.

To anyone not familiar with Singapore, it would seem strange that a self-governing territory attempting to follow the British system of parliamentary democracy should show such scant respect for separating the governmental machinery from that of the party in power. But then Singapore has seldom bothered about the finer points of a liberal democracy.

Mr Lee has himself confessed that he has learnt a lot from his one time association with the Communists. The point he has learnt is to grasp every opportunity with both hands and drive home his advantage time and time again, through the Press and over the wireless and television. He has done precisely this over the Malaysia negotiations.

Having acquired more than a modicum of unpopularity among Singapore's proverbially radical people by staging last year's referendum, he set out to change his image. For months Mr Lee has been devoting every single Sunday to visiting rural constituencies—admittedly his weakest points, as the referendum proved. He walked in slush with trousers rolled up, donned different headgear to please different communities, made promises of street lighting and water pumps.

In spite of the sceptics who scoffed, Mr Lee's country outings won for him some goodwill. A State Prime Minister visiting village homes is a well-worn gambit that seldom fails. But Mr Lee's bigger problem was to conclude the Malaysia agreement in London on the right note.

Financial differences between Singapore and Malaya offered just the opportunity. There is an obvious conflict of interests in a rich city like Singapore joining a largely rural hinterland like Malaya. Such differences can either be magnified or minimized. Mr Lee chose to magnify them, launching an attack at the same time on the Malayan Chinese Association. By coincidence, the MCA President is also the Malayan Finance Minister and thus provided Mr Lee with a perfect target. From then on it was a simple exercise to depict himself as one fighting doggedly for Singapore's interests. It was even announced over the Government-owned Radio Singapore that Mr Lee would either sign the Malaysia agreement or open separate constitutional talks in London on the island's future.

The Malaysia agreement has now been signed and in the eyes of a considerable number of Singapore citizens, Mr Lee has given a good account of himself. This exercise is preliminary to what is coming—the elections.

State elections are due next year but Mr Lee is apparently planning to hold elections for the 15 seats in the Malaysian Parliament allotted to Singapore. He has already announced his intention of contesting this "little election". Although the Malaysian Constitution has yet to be published, a person can presumably be a member of the Federal Parliament and the State Assembly—such is the case in Malaya.

Much will, of course, depend upon the results of the "little election", but Mr Lee will prove to be a formidable opponent, as the Singapore Opposition parties know to their cost. The MCA is one of the members of the Alliance Party in Malaya and recently made an entry into Singapore politics through an alliance composed of the United Malays National Organization and the Malayan Indian Congress plus the Singapore People's Alliance.

Neither Mr Lee's People's Action Party nor the MCA can win the support of the hard-core Leftists. Both parties will therefore try to woo the *towkays* and the small Chinese trader. The new alliance will have the advantage of collecting a number of Indian and Malay votes on a racial basis. Besides, the SPA leader, Mr Lim Yew Hock, a former Singapore Chief Minister who blotted his copybook by his Government's handling of the notorious communal riots of the mid-fifties, is reported to have received the blessing of Tengku Abdul Rahman.

The once powerful Barisan Socialist Party is in sad disarray. Its real leaders, including the popular Mr Lim Chin Siong, are in prison and Mr Lee's tactical victories of the last few months have had a further dampening effect on its supporters. Barisan, however, is still a force in Singapore and can revive, given its leaders any new enthusiasm. Lately, the Barisan has been expending much energy on issuing a flood of statements. The last in the series accuses Mr Lee of being a dictator and ironically refers to him as His Highness Lee Kuan Yew and Emperor Lee Kuan Yew. Consistency is not a strong point of any of Singapore's political parties.

The only other party of note is Mr Ong Eng Guan's United People's Party. Mr Ong, a former Mayor of Singapore, has been tipped as the dark horse who might become Singapore's Prime Minister by the major parties' default. Apparently, Mr Ong himself subscribes to this view but he has not particularly distinguished himself in the exchanges he has had with the PAP and the Barisan. The colourful Mr David Marshall is now partyless and is given to telling friends and acquaintances: "The people of Singapore, it seems, do not want an honest Government."

Man for man, only the detained Mr Lim Chin Siong is a match for Mr Lee. He is unlikely to be released and Mr Lee therefore can well emerge the winner.

15

Roads from two countries led to Manila at the end of July. President Soekarno and Tengku Abdul Rahman journeyed to the Philippines to meet President Macapagal at a summit to give concrete shape to Maphilindo.

It was, however, apparent to everyone that Malaysia was *the* issue before the meeting. Indonesia's renewed opposition to the proposed Federation after the sweetness shed by the cloying Foreign Ministers' conference recommendations in June was a damper to soaring Filipino hopes. Malaya was rather perplexed by, and almost resigned to, Indonesian opposition to Malaysia.

The three heads of Governments are very different in their make-up. President Soekarno has a magnetic and extrovert personality. The Tengku somewhat deliberately creates the impression of a happy-go-lucky man. President Macapagal is shrewd in assessing his own objectives but is feeling his way in regional politics.

The achievement of the Manila summit was that it took place and, having taken place, formally accepted a set of principles for Maphilindo—President Macapagal, in his closing speech, termed it flamboyantly as the Declaration of Independence. The fact that the conference also settled the Malaysia issue after a fashion may prove to be its undoing. The irony of it was that without this settlement, there would have been no Maphilindo.

What role dimly lit tables at seaside night clubs played in bringing about the settlement, as suggested by a Manila wag, is open to question. Manila is particularly geared to providing relaxation and the two visiting delegations, as also their hosts, did justice to the facilities offered.

The three heads of Governments were in search of a solution for very different reasons. President Macapagal had somewhat self-consciously donned the mantle of the peace-maker, pushing into the background in the process his country's claim to North Borneo. President Soekarno, who wanted a temporary settlement for urgent political and economic factors at home, wanted peace on the best possible Indonesian terms. Malaya was prepared to purchase peace and Malaysia if the price was not too high.

The problem therefore was to reconcile Malayan and Indonesian terms for peace. The meeting point ultimately was a vague agreement by which Malayans understand that UN working teams will go to the two Borneo territories of Sabah (North Borneo) and Sarawak to assess the fairness of recent elections there. But the relevant clause of the Manila agreement says that the ascertainment of the wishes of the Borneo people should be made by U Thant or his representative by a "fresh approach" and in "complete compliance" with a General Assembly resolution regarding integration of territories. The UN Secretary-General is to take "into consideration" the recent elections and verify their character.

Malaya made the substantial concession that Malaysia's formation would be dependent upon the UN assessment in Borneo (thus in effect postponing Malaysia), an issue on which she had been hedging for a long time. She also partially gave in to a persistent Indonesian attempt to have the three countries represented on the UN working teams. The three countries, it was decided, would have observers to witness the UN assessment.

A different phraseology has been used in the agreement on the question of observers. The three heads of Governments say it would be "desirable" to have observers from the three countries to witness the UN assessment. This does not form part of the main clause seeking the UN Secretary-General's help in assessing Borneo opinion. Indonesians and Filipinos, however, are inclined to consider the whole agreement as a package deal and would certainly raise objections if an attempt were made to separate the different parts.

The vagueness of the agreement saved Indonesia's face to the extent of enabling her to represent that Malaysia's formation would be dependent upon a UN "referendum". There is confusion in Indonesian minds about the difference between a referendum and a plebiscite. But it also opens the way for Indonesia to exert pressures on the United Nations to thwart Malaysia. Since she has succeeded in internationalizing the issue, the scope for diplomatic manoeuvre is considerable. The introduction of Indonesian observers into the scene can also be used to cause delay.

If the UN Secretary-General does say within about six weeks that he is satisfied with the report of the UN working teams, Indonesia and the Philippines will have little option but to accept Malaysia. If the working teams' verdict is not as clear-cut, there will presumably have to be a plebiscite and Malaysia's future will hang in the balance.

U Thant had nominated Mr Alfred Mackenzie, a UN technical expert stationed in Manila, to liaise with the summit. As messages were exchanged between Manila and New York on the time a UN assessment in the Borneo territories would take (the time shortening with the mode desired), Mr Mackenzie himself became the subject of Indonesian and Filipino suspicions. It was felt in some quarters that he was under Western pressure and was allegedly influencing the UN to favour the Malayans. The fact that U Thant happened to be in Moscow at that time, leaving Mr C.V. Narasimhan in charge, seemed to confirm their suspicions. (Mr Narasimhan's name arouses immediate Indonesian hostility.) Mr Mackenzie was in the unhappy position of being thrust into high pressure politics without the background or talent for the job.

The British role during the conference was also a subject of controversy. A British Foreign Office statement about the inviolability of August 31 as Malaysia Day was an unhappy exercise in diplomacy. Besides, the British Charge d'Affaires in Manila, Mr Theo Peters, made several calls on the Tengku, who was staying in the Presidential suite of Manila Hotel. Few meetings in Manila could have been kept secret, least of all in Manila Hotel, but it was perhaps unnecessary to make a very public demonstration of British interest in the talks.

As Malayan tactics changed from the soft to the hard linc following a Peters visit, Indonesian and Filipino negotiators drew their own conclusions. Britain's interest, however, was legitimate. The two Borneo territories are British and Britain still exercised sovereignty over Singapore. Moreover, by signing the London agreement in July, Malaya had committed itself to the new Federation's formation on August 31. British policy makers could not have been happy over the trend of the discussions since Indonesian motives and objectives are viewed with much suspicion by Whitehall. In the end, British diplomatic observers were left with the feeling that Malaya had somewhat unfairly placed Britain in the uncomfortable position of having to agree to decisions made independently of them.

Indonesian tactics at the conference made a fascinating study. Since the three heads of Governments left acrimonious debates to their Foreign Ministers (the second formal meeting of the summit, however, caused irritation among the participants), these tactics were largely used to gain concessions at the Ministerial level. An impressive array of Indonesian officials, including half a dozen Indonesian Ambassadors called to Manila from their posts, did a splendid job selling the Indonesian line in some very unconventional places. Indonesians also gave a holiday air to the conference by donning jaunty hats and going on shopping expeditions.

At the start of the conference, word was spread round that Indonesians were practically packing their bags if Malaya did not become "more reasonable". Then followed the soft line, followed by sharp private and public attacks on Britain. The peace line prevailed in the end. In the conference room, the irrepressible Dr Subandrio had able support from his deputy, Mr Soedjarwo. Malaya's Minister without Portfolio, Mr Khaw Kai Boh, often took a back seat, leaving it to Mr Ghazali bin Shafie to rebut the arguments of Dr Subandrio and the likeable Mr S.P. Lopez, the newly promoted Philippine Foreign Secretary. Indonesians accurately gauged that the Tengku had included Mr Khaw in the negotiating team to commit the Malayan Chinese Association to Maphilindo.

While failure was not on the cards at the summit, none of the three seemed entirely happy with the settlement. For President Macapagal, the agreement enhanced his prestige at home at a time when his Foreign Secretary's dramatic resignation was proving a political liability. The settlement also firmly placed the Philippines on the regional map. Filipino unhappiness stems from the fact that Maphilindo did not take practical shape at the summit but remained an ideal.

Malayan regrets were caused by the necessity of having to compromise on the date of Malaysia's formation and by throwing the future of the projected Federation open to further doubts and uncertainty. Indonesian motives are harder to divine.

Whatever is in store for Maphilindo, few can contest President Macapagal's claim that a new chapter in the history of Asia has been written. Malaysia dwarfed Maphilindo at the summit but the latter is the more important of the two objectives.

The five points enunciated in the Manila Declaration are couched in very general and laudable terms. Even the reference to the "common struggle against colonialism and imperialism in all their forms and manifestations" is so general that it is capable of more than one interpretation. Tengku Abdul Rahman made clear what his interpretation was. Communist imperialism, he said, was more deadly than any form of imperialism.

In the murky atmosphere of the closing of the summit, the three voices did not speak as one, contrary to President Macapagal's assertion. The Philippine President, it is true, introduced appropriate revolutionary jargon to suit the occasion and his national policy. But the Tengku said he preferred rehabilitation to revolution, and it was left to President Soekarno to launch an attack on imperialist countries, a phrase which has only one connotation to the Indonesian mind.

The significance of the occasion, however, was that the three heads of Governments spoke from the same platform after signing a set of documents that committed them—however vaguely—to the concept of Maphilindo, an ideal to bring 140 million people of Malay stock (the minorities in the three countries are seldom mentioned) closer together.

Both President Macapagal and the Tengku conceded to Indonesia the position of the senior-most member of Maphilindo. In terms of population, Indonesia with its 100 million people dwarfs the envisaged Malaysia with its estimated 10 million and the Philippines with its 30 million inhabitants. In a speech in Manila, President Soekarno made a point of telling his audience that Indonesia had 10,000 islands while the Philippines had only 7,000! He also declared that Indonesia possessed the strongest Army, Navy and Air Force in South-East Asia. His explanation for changing the name of the Indian Ocean to Indonesian Ocean was that the ocean was closer to Indonesia. The following day the Tengku made a point of twice referring to the *Indian* Ocean during a speech.

Maphilindo's future cannot be separated from Indonesia's long-term objectives. Individual Indonesians accept with embarrassed gratitude the theory that the choice in South-East Asia 10 or 20 years hence is between Indonesian and Chinese dominance. Obviously, it does not suit Indonesians publicly to subscribe to this view. Maphilindo, meanwhile, can become a vehicle for promoting Indonesian influence in the region.

It was clear at the conference that one of Indonesia's major objectives was to strike at British economic, political and military position in the area. Much was made of an alleged British interest in breaking the talks and during the closing ceremony President Soekarno spoke of those who did not like the summit conference to succeed.

Inside the conference room, Dr Subandrio tried hard to obtain an assurance from Malaya that she would not permit new foreign bases in the proposed Malaysia. Malayan delegates countered by referring to the question of native bases which could also be used for subversion. There are plans for locating a forward base in the Borneo territories after Malaysia's formation and Malaya did not want to give an undertaking on this point.

Put together, the phrases and sentences spread over the three Manila documents represent a considerable measure of Indonesian success in promoting her anti-British line. The most interesting is the following paragraph contained in the Joint Statement:

"The three heads of Government further agreed that foreign bases—temporary in nature—should not be allowed to be used directly or indirectly to subvert the national independence of any of the three countries. In accordance with the principles enunciated in the Bandung declaration, the three countries will abstain from the use of arrangements of collective defence to serve the particular interests of any of the Big Powers."

Strictly speaking, these implicit strictures apply as much, if not more, to the Philippines as to Malaya. The Philippines not only have a defence treaty with the USA but are also members of SEATO and American economic interests are as strongly represented in the Philippines as British interests in Malaya and the Borneo territories.

However, it was Indonesia's policy to chastise Britain in particular for three main reasons. Indonesia's position would not be too secure if both British and American influence were to disappear from the region. The presence of the Seventh Fleet is perhaps a comforting thought to Djakarta. Secondly, Indonesia expects a substantial amount of American development aid and a systematic attack on the American position in a vulnerable region could have only queered the pitch. Besides, Indonesians were working in close co-operation with the Philippines and did not want to embarrass their hosts.

Against the background of the agreement, Filipino officials explain that American bases in the Philippines are temporary since the defence treaty with the USA can be abrogated by giving due notice. They also say that the Philippines are not members of SEATO "because of the interest of any Big Power".

Malayan delegates are understood to have told Indonesians that since Djakarta did not consider Britain as a Big Power, the reference could not be to the Malayan-British defence treaty! The bilateral nature of the treaty was also emphasized although Filipino officials pointed to the fact that there were also Australian and New Zealand troops in Malaya, giving the agreement a collective character.

The most encouraging aspect of the agreement is the emphasis placed on the right of the three countries to maintain their national identities. Perhaps the Indonesian strategy in introducing an anti-British character to the deliberations was to blunt the Indonesian Communist Party's attack on Maphilindo. That the new concept of the coming together of the Malay race will work to the disadvantage of the Chinese in South-East Asia is clear beyond doubt.

There are some suggestions that the USA is looking on Maphilindo with approval in view of the advantages it could provide in stopping the corrosion of a sensitive area by the Chinese. Indications from Djakarta also suggest that the Soviet Union is not hostile to the concept. Indonesia seems willing to help stop Chinese influence in South-East Asia on its own terms.

16

The story of how Harry Stonehill, an American serviceman turned business man, built up an economic empire worth US$ 250 million in the Philippines and wove a "web of corruption" involving some of the highest in the land is a modern saga of Philippine politics. The interesting point is not that Mr Stonehill made millions but that he could boast of perhaps the most colourful "payroll" of 20th century.

Following investigations into the Stonehill firms by 42 teams of secret service men, President Macapagal ordered the deportation of Mr Stonehill and the resignation of two of his Cabinet Ministers and 15 senior Government officials.

This was in August last year but the name of Stonehill became something of a curse for many men in public life; even a rumoured association with him was sufficient to blight a political career.

The heyday of Mr Stonehill's reign—such it was because he was more powerful than many a modern king—coincided with the Nacionalista Administration, the present Opposition party in the Philippines. It was, therefore, politically advantageous for President Macapagal to pry open some of the secrets of the opposition through Mr Stonehill.

But the President's motives in daring to investigate Mr Stonehill's affairs seem to have been more than merely partisan. (Mr Stonehill had apparently also contributed liberally to Liberal Party funds.) Even before he became President, Mr Macapagal had been trying to build up an image of himself as a man who could give the country an honest Administration—strictly construed, a revolutionary concept in Filipino political life.

The obvious action for the President on assuming office was therefore to strike at merchants of graft and corruption. It is to Mr Macapagal's credit that he did not flinch from investigating Mr Stonehill's affairs. The fantastic array of people who were, in one way or another, beholden to Mr Stonehill made stranger-than-fiction reading.

But a public devouring names with much avidity was kept in unbearable suspense by Mr Macapagal's decision not to reveal all the names contained in the Blue Book, a diary in which Mr Stonehill apparently recorded with meticulous care the names of those beholden to him. Moreover, 16 pages of the Blue Book were reported to be missing and the President rather hurriedly deported Mr Stonehill while many charges were pending against him.

The Macapagal Administration has not been able to explain satisfactorily why Mr Stonehill was so expeditiously sent out of the country. The opposition Nacionalista Party, of course, helped spread the report that Mr Macapagal had bitten off more than he could chew, and deported the American when too many of his own men were becoming involved.

After raging for many months as the biggest political scandal in the history of modern Philippines, the Stonehill legend lay dormant for some time. However, in July Mr Jose Diokno, a former Justice Secretary in Mr Macapagal's Cabinet, resuscitated it. By purporting to produce photostat copies, Mr Diokno tried to implicate the President himself in the Stonehill whirlpool on the strength of an alleged entry made in the name of "V. P. Macapagal". (Mr Macapagal was formerly Vice-President.)

This allegation has, of course, been hotly denied but Mr Stonehill has again become the central obsession of the Philippines. Shortly after Mr Diokno's act, Mr Macapagal's Justice Secretary, Mr Salvador Marino, went on television to recite a list of names figuring in Mr Stonehill's papers. The list included the Vice-President and Foreign Secretary, Mr Emmanuel Pelaez.

Mr Pelaez's reaction was volcanic. He resigned from the Foreign Secretaryship, launching at the same time an onslaught on the "dictatorial" predilections of the President (Mr Pelaez still retains the Vice-Presidency which is, after the American pattern, an elected post). In spite of the President's requests and entreaties, Mr Pelaez has refused to take back his resignation.

I was in Manila on the evening of July 26 when Mr Pelaez addressed a dinner meeting of a business group on the issue of his resignation. Political battles in Manila are fought over dinner and luncheon meetings and before television cameras. Mr Pelaez made a good case for decency in Government although the length to which he went to clear his own name necessarily weakened his impact. Mr Pelaez said his deal with one of Mr Stonehill's firms was perfectly legal and above board.

Mr Pelaez's theory of the attempt to involve him with Mr Stonehill (another name recited was of General Carlos Romulo, former President of the UN General Assembly, who has also filed a suit against Mr Marino) was that by giving the names of acknowledged honest men, the Administration's purpose was to minimize public doubts about "some other people" mentioned in the Stonehill papers. This is a plausible theory and it was apparently Mr Macapagal's intention to clear Mr Pelaez's name publicly, but the latter refused to play the game.

Mr Stonehill, however, has become a symbol of modern Philippines in more senses than one. He was the starting point of Mr Macapagal's "moral regeneration drive". No one I met in the Philippines, including the President's critics, expressed doubts about the President's personal honesty (a rare tribute in Filipino political life). The present controversy centres round the allegation that Mr Macapagal, during his Vice-Presidency, accepted money for his party for fighting elections.

Inevitably, Mr Stonehill has become mixed up in the cross-fire between the Liberal and Nacionalista parties. With Senate elections due in November (Mr Diokno is a Nacionalista candidate), both sides are extracting as much ammunition as they can out of the Stonehill legend.

Mr Pelaez's problem is to stretch the issue of his resignation till the Presidential elections in 1965. It is assumed in Manila that Mr Pelaez is setting his sights on the Presidency. So far the Vice-President has denied rumours of his joining the Opposition Nacionalista Party, but much can happen before 1965.

The Stonehill legend has frayed the temper of another contender to the Presidency, Mr Ferdinand Marcos, the

Liberal Party chairman. His name was also recited by Mr Macapagal's Justice Secretary. Mr Marcos declared that his deal with a Stonehill firm was legitimate. Mr Marcos stood down for Mr Macapagal during the party's nomination for the Presidential candidate on the assurance that he would be nominated for 1965.

Mr Marcos is a young but shrewd politician who can read into the President's actions his desire to run for a second term. Although he seems resigned to let Mr Macapagal have his way, Mr Stonehill might have helped to queer the pitch.

It is typical of the political climate in Manila that a leading Liberal Party leader interpreted the success of the three-nation summit conference to me in the following words: "It will help clean some of the stains left by Mr Stonehill on Mr Macapagal."

17

In many ways, the Brunei revolt of December last year is an object lesson in how not to conduct a revolution. One of the mysteries that remains unexplained is why the rebels chose to fritter away their resources by capturing the oil town of Seria and the adjacent Kuala Belait instead of accomplishing the one task that would have paid them dividends.

The Sultan's palace stands in an isolated part of Brunei Town and the obvious plan to win an insurrection would have been to take the Sultan away to a jungle hideout and issue statements in his name. What happened at the start of the insurrection can at best be described as a half-hearted attempt to spirit the Sultan away.

An ingenious explanation I heard in Djakarta was that the revolt was triggered off too early by British agents working within the "North Borneo National Army". This would lead us somewhere but for the fact that the British were too surprised and distressed by the revolt for the argument to carry conviction. And it still leaves the main question unanswered: why did the rebels behave as they did even if their plans had to be advanced by weeks or months?

Mr Azahari sojourned in Manila during the revolt, but his stay—which started with a bang—ended somewhat in a whimper. For one thing, he lost his associate, Mr Zaini, who defected to the British after painting the town red. Mr Azahari himself carried little conviction with his ceaseless flow of statements as it became apparent that they did not square up with reality.

Not many tears were shed when Mr Azahari left Manila for Djakarta, and on the way—so it was given out—he was parachuted into North Borneo from a civil aircraft. Apparently, he did reach Djakarta and, according to one account I heard in Manila, he was secretly taken out of the Indonesian capital in a food van. The present whereabouts of Mr Azahari are another of Brunei revolt's unexplained mysteries.

Official sources in Singapore say there are at present, in August, only some 85 rebels left in Brunei and they are operating in scattered groups in the jungles. There are between 3,000 and 4,000 British troops in the British Borneo territories and most of them are charged with mopping up operations. The troops' main target is Jassin Affandy, believed to be the main organizer of the revolt, whose head carries a price of M$ 15,000. Curfews, air strikes and tracker dogs have failed to get the last of the rebels to surrender.

To those who wondered why the rebels did not study their primer—they did not take control of Brunei Town's radio station at the start of the revolt—an answer has belatedly been given. A radio station calling itself the Voice of Freedom Fighters of Kalimantan Utara has been broadcasting daily on the 25.2 metre band. Radio experts in Singapore say this station is operating from Djakarta's outskirts or from Indonesian Borneo because a transmitting station of its strength would have to rely on a permanent mains supply, and this could not be done in any of the British Borneo territories without being detected.

Leaving this issue to the experts, the eloquent and vituperative prose being broadcast by the pirate radio every day is worth study. The radio claims to speak for the Government of the Unitary State of Kalimantan Utara which, it says, comprises the three territories of North Borneo, Brunei and Sarawak. The Sultan of Brunei has been proclaimed the Head of State and Mr Azahari its Prime Minister. This is in line with what Mr Azahari propagated in Brunei before the revolt—that Brunei should recapture the past by turning its ruler into a head of the three territories.

The national banner proclaimed is "in the form of the head of a buffalo with three small yellow stars above it and a large yellow star to top them". The buffalo head is a symbol of Brunei's Party Rakyat—now declared illegal. According to the political manifesto broadcast by the radio, the State will follow a neutral and active foreign policy, "send our children to foreign countries to study in various fields", introduce a special law to protect the interests of the workers, raise the living standard of the people, protect minority interests and form an Army, Navy and Air Force and Police Force "with the most modern weapons".

The radio issues blandishments, threats, warnings, appeals and morale-boosters. Sometimes there is a desperate edge to appeals: "For us there is no road left but to fight to the last man in order to drive away the British colonialists from our land". Sometimes an attitude of defiance: "Our soldiers are everywhere and they follow the movements of the sun's rays in the jungle; they are behind every log, every tree and in the mountains". Sometimes a promise to "firmly protect" British interests in exchange for British recognition; at other times a threat to give away "British concessions" to other foreign Powers who give the "Government" moral and material support.

The radio makes no secret of the particular inspiration it draws from the Indonesian example. It has proclaimed Malay as the "State's" national language on the strength of Indonesian success in this field. At other times, it appeals to Indonesia to do more for the "struggle of the people of Kalimantan Utara" since time is running out. The object of the radio's particular hatred is the Malayan Prime Minister.

The plaints of the Voice of Freedom Fighters amount to an effort to keep alive in the political sphere a revolt that failed on the ground. The 85 or more who have not surrendered are doing their bit to lend substance to some of the flamboyant protestations of the pirate radio.

18

At midnight of September 15-16 the new nation of Malaysia came into being after more than a year of trials and tribulations.

Lavish celebrations are being planned in Kuala Lumpur, the Federal capital, and in the other constituent units of the new nation, but the note of jubilation is marred by the Indonesian decision not to recognize Malaysia for the present and uncertainty about future Indonesian moves.

The Pan-Malayan Islamic Party controlled State of Kelantan is not joining in in the celebrations and vainly tried to frustrate Malaysia on a technical ground in an eleventh hour petition to the Supreme Court. In Penang island, the Socialist Front controlled City Council refused to make appropriate arrangements for the celebrations as a gesture of protest against Malaysia's formation.

Singapore is decked with flags and bunting, welcome arches and a million lights, but everyone is more concerned about snap general elections set by Mr Lee Kuan Yew for September 21 than with Malaysia.

There is general recognition in Singapore and Kuala Lumpur that Malaysia's troubles are not over with its formation. But Tengku Abdul Rahman and his colleagues in the Federal capital can take a measure of credit for the mere fact of its existence. The proposal to have the new Federation triggered off a revolt in Brunei, which has chosen to stay out, worsening relations between Malaya on one hand and Indonesia and the Philippines on the other and led to a polarization of political forces in the country.

In a sense, the regional crisis created by Malaysia's formation was responsible for the executive heads of Malaya, Indonesia and the Philippines getting together in Manila and giving their formal approval to a Maphilindo confederation. The present is not the moment for Maphilindo but the future might well see the concept bloom into a compelling ideal.

Malaysia's immediate worries are to watch its land frontier with Indonesia in the jungles of Sarawak for signs that the present trickle of guerrillas does not become a flood. On the political plane, a continuing confrontation by Indonesia would cause many crises between two countries which have racial, religious and family ties.

It does not seem likely that in view of her troubles at home Indonesia will commit a substantial portion of her forces in a guerrilla war in Sarawak. Besides, it is one thing to try to prevent a new Federation from coming into being and quite another to try to break it. Reasons for Indonesian dislike and distrust of Malaysia are many and deepseated.

Politically, Indonesia distrusts a new entity which is very closely linked with Britain, militarily and otherwise, and considers Malaysia an affront to her ambitions for Big Power status in the area. Years of bickering with Malaya and the ideological differences involved, combined with Indonesia's own problems of keeping thousands of scattered islands together, have not helped matters.

Britain's key role in helping to bring the Federation into being has therefore not been exactly welcome to Indonesia. Ironically, a process of decolonization initiated by Britain has become hateful to an anti-colonial Government—U Thant's endorsement notwithstanding.

19

Ash Wednesday they call it in Djakarta, the burning of the British Embassy on September 18 and the sacking of British homes. The chancellery building is a mere shell with blackened holes and twisted window frameworks jutting out in a grim surrealistic pattern.

Outside the British Ambassador's house near by are scrawled in white paint the words, *Imperialis Inggris*. This legend is frequently repeated at street corners with others, such as "Tengku No, Azahari Yes" and similar incantations against Malaysia. Near the President's Palace, the board announcing the British Council's office has the word British crossed out violently in red paint.

What happened in Djakarta on Ash Wednesday will live long in some memories. After months of intense anti-British propaganda came the burning of the chancellery, the systematic sacking of British homes, the overturning of British cars which were then set on fire. No one was hurt. In each house the residents were ordered out and their belongings smashed and burned. An element of terror the situation created for those at the receiving end was undeniable.

Panic spread. The British sought shelter in Hotel Indonesia because their homes were unlivable and considered unsafe. Shelter was given, after official intervention. By a curious twist of fate, this solitary modern hotel in Djakarta stands opposite the then-smouldering chancellery building. Evacuation of British women and children began. The Australian Ambassador decided to follow suit, a decision of Mr Keith Shann's that has drawn fire from his home country as a panicky move. It obviously had the effect of embarrassing the Indonesian Government which wanted to single out the British for displeasure.

Other embassies did not evacuate dependents but a nervousness persists among members of many diplomatic missions. Deprived of their homes and families, British diplomats and business men continue to live in Hotel Indonesia (it has yet to be determined at whose expense) and try to forget their individual losses over glasses of whisky. The hotel bar is now jocularly called the Union Jack Club.

No one who has witnessed recent events can doubt that they were organized by the authorities. There is room for debate as to whether all that happened was planned but all of it seems to have been authorized at the time of its occurrence. Indonesian officials have been vainly suggesting that Major Walker's bagpipes (in itself a foolish act) constituted a provocation for the crowds. If so, the policemen on duty did precious little to try to restore order.

The human aspects of the situation, in terms of the suffering caused and the methods adopted to cause them, seem to have made very little impact on the Indonesian leaders. Individual Indonesians have felt ashamed, some make bold to say so privately. But the general Indonesian reaction seems to be that the British have got what they deserved.

To an extent, the economic confrontation of Malaysia and the anti-British riots constituted an emotional reaction to the announcement of the new date for Malaysia's formation, U Thant's conclusions on the Borneo territories and the Federation's birth. There are indications that President Soekarno was not kept fully informed of world events and the trend of events perhaps gave Indonesian leaders the feeling of being humiliated.

By themselves, demonstrations organized against a European Power in an Asian country do not represent a crisis. But with Indonesia, for long considered a problem child in many Western and other chancelleries, they came at a singularly unfortunate moment. Economic reform measures were beginning to have effect. There were prospects of a reasonable level of Western aid flowing into the country. And, with the prospect of an Indonesian-dominated Maphilindo taking shape in the future, it was generally assumed that Indonesia would tone down its militancy to consolidate the economic gains. The anti-British riots have changed this picture.

Indonesian leaders are quick to grasp reality when they want to, and their new conciliatory gestures and relative calm flow from a recognition of the untoward consequences that can flow from recent events. The Djakarta District Governor has promised to help rebuild the British chancellery and Britons whose homes have been sacked have been asked to register their claims individually. Between promise and fulfilment, however, lies a chasm of uncertainty.

At British prodding, members of Djakarta's diplomatic corps met to debate British charges that despite repeated requests made to the Foreign Office, Indonesians had refused to give British diplomatic establishments adequate protection. The corps, including the Soviet representative, decided to draw Djakarta's attention to the Vienna conventions on diplomatic immunity. The Chinese Ambassador in Djakarta paid the meeting the unusual courtesy of officially excusing himself.

The role the U.S. Ambassador, Mr Howard Jones, had to play was a delicate one. As dean of the diplomatic corps, he had to make strong protests over the happenings. These protests, however, did not always square up with his own punctilious efforts to keep Indonesian-U.S. relations on a relatively cordial level. But Mr Jones managed to keep his national and international identities separate although he did not entirely please the British in the process.

Present Indonesian efforts are directed at reducing its relative isolation in the international community. It is for this reason that the strong statement made by Sir Robert Menzies, the Australian Prime Minister, that Australia should come to Malaysia's aid in case of attack or subversion from outside failed to draw Indonesian ire. The Indonesian Foreign Minister, Dr Subandrio, told me in Djakarta in September that Indonesian-Australian difficulties were temporary.

In spite of the proddings of the Indonesian Communist Party, not a stone has been aimed at U.S. diplomatic offices in Djakarta during the troubles. And there have been some pungent things said about Indonesia in the USA. The semi-official *Indonesian Herald*, in fact, made a point of lauding Mr Jones.

The statement of Mrs Lakshmi Menon, India's junior Foreign Minister, in Kuala Lumpur in September that Indonesia and the Philippines had gone back on their word by not accepting U Thant's findings caused much nervousness among the Indian community in Djakarta. But it was allowed to be forgotten and, in spite of it, President Soekarno paid a very unusual visit to the Indian Ambassador's residence to participate in a Gandhi memorial ceremony specially arranged for him on October 3, a day after the annual ceremonies were performed.

I was at the receiving end of Indonesia's economic confrontation of Malaysia. On my return trip from Djakarta to Singapore in October, it took 12 hours, including a wait and change of planes at Bangkok, to cover a distance which normally takes 1½ hours by jet.

No airline is allowed to pick up passengers or freight destined for Malaysia and *vice versa.* This order also applies to shipping and the trade boycott of Malaysia, as far as Indonesia is concerned, is technically complete.

This has caused immense problems for traders as well as others. In Sumatra, crude rubber is piling up and smallholders, who produce most of Indonesia's rubber, are affected. In Djakarta, offices are short of paper, scotch tape and other humble articles of daily use.

There has been a sudden slump in parties in Djakarta whose diplomatic corps is even more addicted to giving and attending parties than New Delhi's. Duty free supplies of liquor, cigarettes and canned food, normally emanating from or routed through Singapore, are at a low ebb.

Indonesians are right when they call their economic confrontation a blessing in disguise. But the disguise is thick and was perhaps not entirely necessary. The pattern of trade between Indonesia and what is now Malaysia is such that it could never satisfy a growing independent country. Singapore and Penang have been the traditional processors of Indonesian raw materials and its middlemen.

It stands to reason that middlemen will charge a price for their business efficiency and processing plants. It is equally true that a producer of raw materials does not love the middleman. The logical method of reducing its great economic dependence on Malaysia would have been for Indonesia to consolidate its economy and to build plants to process its own rubber and smelt its own tin and to raise an entrepreneur class of its own. This is of necessity a slow process.

Singapore estimates of annual imports into Singapore and Malaya from Indonesia are of the order of M$ 1,000 million and exports to Indonesia of M$ 300 million. Indonesian estimates are more conservative. One figure of the two-way annual trade between Indonesia and Malaysia quoted in Djakarta was M$ 800 million. Since smuggling plays a substantial part in the two-way trade, these figures are at best approximations.

Some six months ago there were definite indications that, in spite of the habitual play it continued to make in the political field, Indonesia was taking necessary steps to begin economic development in earnest. However, having been caught on the wrong foot in the final act of Phase I of the Malaysia dispute, the Indonesian reaction was to make economic considerations subservient to those of political prestige and emotionalism.

Indonesians are now trying to make a virtue of necessity. But in a very real sense, launching economic confrontation has solved at one stroke a very big problem confronting Indonesia. After years of political indoctrination, which was necessary in many ways, the Indonesian people have been conditioned to a set of reflex actions all of which are politically motivated. The transition from slogan shouting and fighting guerrilla wars to building up an economy is necessary but difficult to accomplish.

Even six months ago there was little realization among Indonesians of the need to do something positive about the economy, except to make political capital out of it. The picture has now been dramatically altered. This is, of course, only the beginning of a new indoctrination programme which will propagate a new set of doctrines. Indonesia will succeed to the extent it can devote itself singlemindedly to propagating and implementing economic doctrines without yielding inordinately to the temptation of keeping alive its psychological war with Malaysia.

Indonesians have a tremendous capacity for displaying optimism in face of adversity. The odds, for the present and immediate future, are immense. American aid is expected to continue to flow into Indonesia at the annual level of some U.S.$ 70 million—this would include shipments of rice and cotton. But the American sponsorship of international consortium aid to help Indonesia's balance of payments position is now an open question. Getting the U.S. Congress to approve more economic aid for Indonesia will prove to be a very difficult problem.

Japan however has chosen to honour its commitment of U.S.$ 12 million under the Development Assistance Committee plan. The visit to Indonesia of the Japanese Prime Minister, Mr Ikeda, in September would not have been made had it been decided otherwise. Increasingly cordial ties are developing between these two countries and the Japanese are keenly alive to the economic potentialities Indonesia holds for them.

Indonesian Cabinet Ministers are inclined to wave off difficulties with a nonchalant smile and unfurl new plans, necessarily tentative for the present, for meeting the situation. There are differences in the Cabinet on the pace at which economic confrontation should proceed with one section, led by Dr Djuanda, favouring a more conventional approach than Mr Chairul Saleh's. It is expected to take some months before a new economic programme is hammered out. The formation of three task forces, after the Indonesian fashion, has been announced.

Having lost for the present a substantial portion of the U.S.$ 250 million DAC aid, Indonesia is determined to secure a further deferment of repayment on Russian arms. Efforts are also being made to get U.S.$ 50 million from the International Monetary Fund. At the same time Indonesia is offering to trade directly with the rest of the world, hoping to offset the loss of efficiency and traditional trading arrangements by quoting lower prices.

Economic competition in the world being what it is, there are takers. A tin smelting agreement has been signed between Indonesia and Holland. The Dutch are re-entering the Indonesian market with relish but are displaying supreme caution in Djakarta, believing in the adage that they should be seen but not heard. Responsible Indonesians say that the Dutch have assured them of trade and aid.

The West Germans have been displaying a certain nervousness over the re-entry of the Dutch. A love hate relationship continues to operate between the Indonesians and the Dutch, and generations of habit make Indonesians favour Dutch products—Indonesian city dwellers, for instance, sorely miss Dutch cheese. The Germans therefore have reasons to fear that they might lose the markets they once gained from the Dutch. Indonesians have, however, assured them that they will keep what they have.

The main reason for the continuing British presence in Indonesia is economic. British investments in the country are estimated at £ 160 million although Indonesians say that this figure is "50% exaggerated". Both Britain and Indonesia make a distinction between oil and other interests. By recently signing a new oil agreement with Djakarta (obviously with Whitehall approval), Shell considerably constrained official British action. Indonesians seem to be interested in keeping oil production going but the future of other British firms is clouded.

These and other arrangements, as for instance the new trade agreement with the Philippines, will only solve a fraction of the colossal problems raised by economic confrontation. Indonesians are realistic enough to recognize that smuggling between Indonesia and Malaysia cannot be stopped. They are also turning a blind eye to Panamanian ships reportedly carrying freight between Singapore and Djakarta. The Bank of Indonesia is continuing to operate in Singapore and a Singapore trade agency continues to function temporarily in Djakarta.

To the question whether Indonesia is serious about its economic confrontation policy there is no simple answer. Economic confrontation is a new doctrine that will snowball over the years, perhaps to occupy an honoured place among the hoary concepts of Indonesian polity.

Once it has achieved that status it will be for the Indonesian authorities to swing the people in the desired direction. For the present economic confrontation is largely a lever to obtain a temporary political solution in the region.

Indonesian leaders are disarmingly frank about throwing their ideological beliefs to the winds in planning for economic confrontation. It is, for instance, highly ironical that in spite of the great play Indonesia makes about its anti-colonialism, it should have given back to Holland the smelting of tin—thus, in effect, perpetuating the classical concept of Western dominance.

By the same token, by taking away the tin smelting trade from Penang, Indonesia has struck at the roots of the Maphilindo concept which envisaged increased trade between Indonesia, Malaya and the Philippines. The whole concept of economic confrontation is a negation of Maphilindo.

Indonesians also say that they will sacrifice their socialization plans to give incentives to private enterprise in the country. One Cabinet Minister suggested to me that Indonesia could invite the Chinese, from Singapore if necessary, to set up entrepot trade centres! Indonesians justify these steps on grounds of national interest and say they are temporary measures dictated by necessity. Ends, in other words, justify the means.

In so far as economic thinking is crystallizing in Djakarta, it is envisaged to operate a crash programme to set up a string of free ports and entrepot trade centres along the major Indonesian islands. This is obviously to supplant Singapore's position as the entrepot trading centre in South-East Asia and to end Indonesia's own dependence on Singapore.

The feeling sedulously cultivated in Indonesia that the impossible is possible will greatly help this new and growing preoccupation with economic freedom from Malaysia. It should be recognized at the same time that economic planning requires fewer flashes of brilliance and momentary superhuman effort, more of stamina.

While new ideas about economic confrontation are taking shape in Djakarta, realistic plans are also being made on the extent to which the traditional Indonesian-Malaysian trade can be restored if there is a political settlement. It has apparently been decided not to restore the tin smelting trade to Penang. On the refining of Indonesian crude oil in Malaysia the Djakarta authorities are more flexible. But particularly with regard to rubber and other agricultural products, Indonesia would only be happy to go back to Malaysia for the time being.

Rubber in particular is a headache for Djakarta because in view of the elementary methods of rubber production employed and the limited quantities traditionally shipped at one time, its processing and sale present many problems. To the extent the Philippines and other countries can take over the Indonesian rubber and copra and other trade, only to that extent will the Malaysians be denied it.

The climate for a political settlement is more propitious than it has been for some time. Indonesians tend to equate both Malaysia and the Philippines with themselves in discussing the factors responsible for creating the present crisis. For obvious reasons Indonesia does not want to display too much eagerness in seeking a compromise but will grasp any genuine peace offer.

After releasing a fantastic array of trial balloons on an imminent Filipino recognition of Malaysia, Manila is for the moment keeping quiet. The trial balloons were obviously to prepare public opinion for a change in policy, but Manila is acting in consultation with Djakarta and is prepared to resuscitate the Maphilindo concept to save the situation and the ideal.

Diplomatically, Malaysia is in a strong position on the question of its recognition by the other two countries. As evidence of this, Tengku Abdul Rahman has set three conditions before a new three-nation meeting can be held. The most difficult of his conditions is prior recognition of Malaysia. This the other two countries will find difficult to accept before some compromise settlement is reached.

The field has been open for mediators. Japan's tentative efforts at a regional conference have, however, not borne fruit because the proposal has smacked too much of the Japanese "co-prosperity sphere" plan of the last war. Thailand is the only mediator left in the field at present. Thailand's proposal for a three-nation Foreign Ministers' conference in Bangkok (significantly the phrase used is Malay Foreign Ministers' conference) has U.S. support and is a sensible idea. Strictly speaking, if Foreign Ministers of the three countries would meet, even informally, they would be recognizing Malaysia's existence since Malaya ceased to exist on September 16.

The Tengku can perhaps make some concession in this regard. He is not an inflexible man but for the present any obvious concession he were to make would probably be misunderstood by both his own party and Britain.

1964
VIOLENCE, HOPES AND DESPAIR

20

At Kuala Lumpur airport one day in January, the Defence Minister of Malaysia wept as an aircraft brought the bodies of eight Malaysian soldiers killed in an ambush in Borneo. The spectacle of Tun Abdul Razak, a stolid matter-of-fact man, sobbing was a symbol of the country's sense of shock over a unique tragedy.

The incident took place almost on New Year's eve at a timber outpost at Kalabakan in Sabah. Malaysian soldiers were bivouacked in two houses not far from a settlement of Indonesian workers who traditionally provide the labour force for Sabah's booming timber trade. Hand grenades aimed at the houses found eight soldiers dead and 19 wounded. The intruders left after an engagement with the remaining troops and were swallowed up by the surrounding jungle.

Tension along what is now the Malaysian-Indonesian border in Borneo has already claimed over a hundred lives. But never had the wages of Indonesian confrontation tasted as bitter. To the poignancy of those killed being their own flesh and blood was added the circumstance of their death. Tengku Abdul Rahman said it was treachery. The conclusion was, indeed, inescapable that although most terrorists—as the guerrillas in Borneo are officially described—operated from Indonesian bases across the border, there must have been collusion in this case. Kalabakan is 30 miles inside Malaysian territory.

Malaya, the dominant partner of the new Federation of Malaysia, became independent in 1957. There was the war, the Japanese occupation and those 12 dogged years of the Emergency. But the first two events took place before freedom, and the guerrilla war against the Communists was largely won under the British. Recent history has been rather kind to Malaya and its genial Prime Minister has always placed stress on happiness as the main objective for his nation.

Then came the concept of Malaysia, and almost overnight Malaya was swept into the whirlpool of regional politics. Indonesian confrontation of Malaysia alternated with peace talks. Bitter words of abuse have often yielded place to great protestations of friendship. In the public consciousness of Malaya there has always been a Micawber like quality of good fortune (and peace) being round the corner.

Kalabakan has changed this to an extent. It is now being recognized in Kuala Lumpur that Indonesian confrontation represents the first real test for free Malaya, and the other units of Malaysia. Kalabakan is part of the growing up process which is necessary but awkward.

Malaysia's basic problem begins with the composition of its population. An estimated 60% of the Malays are of Indonesian stock and, together with the deep feelings of a common religion and race, share kinship with Indonesians. The presence of two immigrant races in large numbers—the Chinese and the Indian—makes the Malays' attachment to Indonesia the greater.

Indonesian hostility therefore strikes at the root of Malay consciousness. There is an unreal quality about the loud protestations against Indonesia although political expediency has made Kuala Lumpur sponsor them. Malaysians say that the present crisis has helped knit the country's heterogeneous peoples into one nation because the immigrant races' suspicions of Malays' attachment to Indonesia have now been reduced. How lasting this phenomenon will be remains to be seen.

Continuing Indonesian taunts about the British running Malaysia have made Kuala Lumpur more conscious of the important role the British are continuing to play in Government, industry and defence. Malaysians now freely admit that the British are a political liability in Borneo, but they immediately add that, but for them, the Indonesians would have had a field day. And there is an ironical twist in present Malaysian suspicions that, with British troops already overcommitted, London might have second thoughts over fighting an unending guerrilla war in the jungles of Borneo. An interesting indication of these suspicions was a red herring floated in Kuala Lumpur about the virtues of Malaysia joining SEATO.

One can still hear the stock arguments in Kuala Lumpur. How can 10 million Malaysians want to fight 100 million Indonesians? How can Indonesia, with its strong armed forces, fear encirclement? But more thought is being given to more important issues.

There are so many imponderables in the situation that long-term planning has to be based on assumptions. One assumption is that apart from the ideological pull Indonesia will continue to exercise over a section of the people in Malaysian Borneo, subversion from across the border will continue. Increasing attention is therefore being paid to counter-propaganda and a newly expanded external service of Radio Malaysia is trying to reach the high standards in vitriolic prose set by official and other Indonesian radio stations. Malaysian researchers are also digging into history to find incriminating evidence against Indonesia.

From the military point of view, Malaysians will have to continue to rely upon outside help because their own armed forces are too small to be able to defend the country. The 30-year British defence treaty with Malaya, now extended to Malaysia, is the sheet anchor, but many Malaysians hope that their dependence on one European Power were less complete. They would therefore have welcomed Australian and New Zealand support in Borneo and are for the same reason bitter over what they describe as the USA's ambivalent attitude towards Indonesia.

Events culminating in Kalabakan have helped build up a tempo in Malaya and the biggest problem before the leaders in Kuala Lumpur today is to maintain this tempo against the changing tactics of Indonesia. Government leaders feel that they cannot play ducks with the population, with elections due in April or May. Opposition parties will pounce upon the ruling Alliance Government, given half a chance.

How to reconcile this requirement of practical politics with the equally important problem of Malaysia's image abroad is worrying Kuala Lumpur. In so far as the Malaysian crisis is being internationalized, to that extent will Kuala Lumpur need international support and sympathy. Malaysia therefore cannot afford to create the impression of refusing to negotiate a settlement.

21

The U.S. Attorney-General, Mr Robert Kennedy, gives the impression of being a diffident man. He is also unflappable, as he demonstrated during his visit to Kuala Lumpur in January, one of the five Asian capitals he visited during the course of his Malaysia mission.

During a stay of a little over 24 hours in Kuala Lumpur, Mr Kennedy had two memorable sessions with the Press. He exuded sober optimism but refused to be drawn into details.

When a question became too tricky, he simply answered, "I don't think I can comment on that".

The consequences of a failure of the Kennedy mission would have been very grave, and it was recognition of this fact by the three parties to the dispute that helped President Johnson's emissary in his task. But in an atmosphere charged with suspicions and animosities, it would have been only too easy to cause offence. Mr Kennedy not only avoided this in his conversations in the five capitals but was also able to satisfy everyone about his own sincerity.

A part of Mr Kennedy's job was to listen to the set pieces each of the three contestants had to recite. In Kuala Lumpur, Malaysians wanted to tell him how wronged they were and how little encouragement they had received from Washington. In Tokyo, President Soekarno, then holidaying there, was anxious to set the record straight. In Manila, President Macapagal gave an account of what he had done to secure peace. Mr Kennedy proved a good listener although most of what he heard was familiar to him. As the Asian leaders discovered, he had done his homework.

Now that there is a temporary cease-fire on the island of Borneo as a result of Mr Kennedy's mission, the three contestants have been given a breathing space. Their interest in seeking a pause had different motivations. For Indonesia a continuing involvement in what would have become a guerrilla war in Borneo forcing upon the country a dramatic and unwelcome orientation in foreign policy, apart from greater economic difficulties, was a tunnel of no return.

The Philippines, burdened with their luckless claim to Sabah, were beginning to feel increasingly isolated and President Soekarno's visit to Manila in January produced some forebodings about Indonesia. It was perhaps to reduce this feeling of isolation that prompted President Macapagal to inject Prince Sihanouk of Cambodia into the Malaysia crisis at the risk of offending the Thais. The Cambodian Head of State had his own reasons for surprising Kuala Lumpur with a visit in January, at a time it was preparing to receive Mr Kennedy. If the Prince was hoping to meet President Johnson's emissary (Mr Kennedy was decidedly cool to the idea), he was disappointed but undeterred.

Malaysia has been desperately for peace. Its precipitate action in breaking diplomatic relations with Indonesia and the Philippines and the consequent heightening of Indonesian confrontation and a new economic boycott by Djakarta produced a vicious circle. Increasing border incidents in Borneo served to increase pressures on Tengku Abdul Rahman to continue to take a hard line and there were mounting suspicions in Kuala Lumpur of Indonesia's long-term objectives.

Mr Kennedy has now provided the three an occasion to disentangle themselves from their inflexible positions. The cease-fire is an opportunity to reassess tactics although the basic objectives of the three countries will presumably remain the same.

Indonesia's ambition for Big Power status in South-East Asia are known and, up to a point, acceptable. The experience of the last four months however should introduce an element of caution in Djakarta which should have discovered that the flexing of muscles is not a good cover for tactical errors committed. Whether Indonesia will seek to dominate the region through the concept of Maphilindo or be driven off course by internal pressures and contradictions is still not clear.

The Philippines will be having second thoughts on the extent of their commitments to Djakarta, although President Macapagal should have no cause to change his basic policy of friendship with Indonesia. But too close an alignment with a powerful neighbour has its disadvantages, as Manila has discovered. And if President Macapagal wants the Maphilindo concept to flower, he should not give the impression of teaming up with Indonesia against Malaysia at a future summit conference. The first summit produced precisely this impression and Tengku Abdul Rahman later alluded to it in his characteristic manner by saying that Malaya felt like a Cinderella.

Malaya will go to the next conference with Indonesia with greater caution. Kuala Lumpur has necessarily to take a guarded attitude towards Maphilindo in view of the percentage of Chinese population in the country. And Chinese suspicions of Maphilindo's aims have increased in the meantime, while Malays have learnt to distrust Indonesian protestations of friendship.

A final compromise settlement on Malaysia, as and when arrived at, will doubtless be couched in the sonorous phrases of the Manila declarations of last year. But a lot of horse-trading will have to precede a new conference.

The efforts of Tengku Abdul Rahman and President Macapagal at their proposed meeting in Phnom Penh in February will obviously be to evolve a formula for Manila's claim to Sabah. A formula was arrived at towards the end of last year during the ECAFE conference in Bangkok and Malaysians claim that, but for Indonesian intervention, it would have been accepted. Essentially, this consisted of a Malaysian promise to entertain Manila's claim within the limits set by Sabah's integration in Malaysia and U.N. approval for it.

Indonesians will insist on Malaysia getting British troops out of Borneo and an intriguing question that only time can answer is whether they will be prepared to abandon confrontation in return. This concept has perhaps served its usefulness but still remains a handy tool for Indonesia's declared aim of anti-colonialism.

22

The general elections in Malaya, being held on April 25, are important not for their immediate outcome but for the indications they will give of future trends in Malaysia.

It seems reasonably certain that the Alliance Government of Tengku Abdul Rahman will be returned to power. None of the Opposition parties is making a serious attempt to capture the Central Government. Their immediate ambitions are more limited: to try to win one or more States.

Only Malaya is going to the polls for State and Parliamentary elections. The other three units of Malaysia—Singapore, Sarawak and Sabah—have had their elections. The Alliance Government starts with an advantage in having 35 of the 55 seats allotted to these three units in the Malaysian Parliament of 129 members.

The ruling Alliance party in Malaya is an amalgam of three racial units. This reflects the crux of the problem Malaysia's multi-racial texture poses. The parties' ambitions and following are intertwined with the different races and their place in the Malaysian society.

Malays enjoy a dominant political and constitutional position but very little economic power. The Chinese among the non-European races are pre-eminently the holders of wealth and industry. The Indians largely constitute estate labour although there is a fair sprinkling of them in the professions.

Flowing from the broad fact of Malays' political dominance is the restricted nature of citizenship laws for the immigrant races and, consequently, the small total electorate of nearly 2.8 million out of a population of over seven million. A second factor is the relatively high proportion of the young who have not reached voting age.

Although the Alliance is fielding candidates for all the 104 Parliamentary and 282 State Assembly seats under its common label, election issues can only be understood in the racial context. UMNO's chief antagonist is the extreme right-wing Pan-Malayan Islamic Party. As the only Opposition party ruling one of the 11 States of Malaya, PMIP deserves respect. What is more, it enjoys a certain potential advantage in being able to mix religion with politics, and the brew can be a heady mixture for a predominantly rural electorate.

The PMIP is naturally anxious to retain its hold over the central-eastern State of Kelantan and extend it to neighbouring Trengganu, if not further to Kedah on the north-west. UMNO is not unaware of PMIP's appeal and has been lately concentrating its fire power on these States.

The Socialist Front seeks to give a multi-racial character to its socialistic ideas by combining the Chinese-based Labour Party with the Malay-based Party Rakyat—the leader of the latter is detained for his alleged pro-Indonesian activities. The Socialist Front's present aims are confined to capturing the Penang State where a Socialist Front controlled City Council has been serving as an advertisement for the party. A newcomer to the Front is the National Convention Party, fathered by the former Agriculture Minister, Mr Aziz Ishak.

Even more limited in character is the scope of the People's Progressive Party, which has confined its resources to Ipoh and the surrounding areas of the north-western tin-mining State of Perak. The PPP has now combined with the United Democratic Party to try to win Perak State from the Alliance. It is difficult to say what these two parties really stand for; the PPP is not averse to utilizing the resentment of a section of the Chinese and Indians to the political privileges Malays enjoy. The UDP, of fairly recent vintage, in effect serves a similar purpose.

Contrary to earlier indications, Mr Lee Kuan Yew's People's Action Party of Singapore announced some time ago that it would put up a few candidates in the Malayan elections. PAP's entry into Malaya is a symbolic one (it is fielding only nine candidates for Parliament), but this symbol has disturbed many a placid pool of Malayan politics.

After Malaysia's formation, it was generally assumed that Mr Lee would not long remain satisfied with confining his political ambitions to Singapore. Mr Lee's extension to the Malayan scene has come sooner than anticipated. In effect, he is using the present elections to test his strength in a new region before staking his claims in the whole of Malaysia.

Although the PAP has been careful to project an inter-racial image in the candidates it has put up, its real ambition is to replace the Malayan Chinese Association as a partner of UMNO in the Alliance. Besides, there is no love lost between Mr Lee and the MCA leader, Mr Tan Siew Sin.

Election issues in the campaigns and rallies have taken an expected character. Since Indonesia's confrontation of Malaysia touches many political, economic and social aspects of life in Malaya, this has been an obvious issue. The two Opposition parties—PMIP and the Socialist Front—have taken an anti-Malaysia stand. Components of the ruling Alliance have therefore made the confrontation issue their main election plank.

There are obvious advantages for the Alliance in playing up the dangers of Indonesian confrontation and of presenting itself as the only unit which can defend the nation's integrity. In view of the PMIP and SF attitude, they have had to be on the defensive on this point. The bomb scare in Singapore and a well-timed disclosure of an alleged Indonesian plot to assassinate the Tengku have been grist to the

Alliance mill. The PMIP, on the other hand, is largely relying on its religious and frankly racial appeal for the rural Malay voter. The Socialist Front is banking on its image in Penang's City Council and hopes to mop up the radical Chinese votes to win the State.

The Alliance has publicized its record of the last five years in administration, finance, diplomacy and economic development. Much attention has been paid by UMNO leaders to rural development, for the good reason that the bulk of Malay voters live in the country. The MCA leader, Mr Tan Siew Sin, has stressed, in rather conventional arguments, the Government's good husbandry. The MIC, on the other hand, is the only component of the Alliance without a racial rival.

Since Mr Lee's main interest in the present elections is to project a suitable image of himself, he has been careful in choosing his planks. For one thing, he has posed himself as the harbinger of the "winds of change". More concretely, he has promised to begin a "social and economic revolution" and has highlighted Singapore's impressive achievements in public amenities and housing—something the PAP promises to repeat in Malaya.

This judicious mixture of the concrete and the abstract is obviously directed at the Chinese voter who is essentially the town and city dweller; the Malay largely resides in the country. This strategy has brought upon Mr Lee the charge from UMNO leaders that he is "driving a wedge" between the two races. With the MCA leaders, Mr Lee has been conducting an endless debate laced with pithy epithets. He has in fact been careful not to annoy UMNO more than he can help while concentrating his vitriolic prose for the MCA and the opposition Malayan parties.

So much attention has been paid to the People's Action Party by the ruling and opposition parties in Malaya that at times it gave the impression of PAP fighting the rest. The MCA leaders seem worried about the potential threat to their position the PAP poses. UMNO leaders are frankly unhappy at seeing a dynamic Chinese leader entering their political arena from Singapore.

23

The end of Malayan general elections has set off a chain reaction in many capitals in South-East Asia. From Indonesia, cries of crush Malaysia and double commands have mingled with conciliatory Indonesian-style statements that Djakarta was "not begging for *musjawarah* (consultations)" if Tengku Abdul Rahman did not want to negotiate on the Malaysia crisis.

In Manila, optimistic assessments of the future have been expressed optimistically. In Tokyo, the Japanese Foreign Minister has been trying to maintain a Japanese balance between his country's affections for Indonesia and Malaysia.

From Kuala Lumpur, Tengku Abdul Rahman has demonstrated that intemperate remarks are not a monopoly of Indonesia. After his election victory, he reportedly answered a correspondent's question by declaring, "To hell with Soekarno".

The visit of the British Foreign Secretary, Mr. Butler, to Tokyo in April became largely a Malaysia mission. Among other things, it served to underline the differences between Tokyo and London in their approach to the Malaysia crisis. Since Britain is the most involved third party in the dispute, she is handicapped in making a move for reconciliation, although any significant change in London's assumptions about Indonesia would help.

Australia, meanwhile, has been drawn closer to British thinking on the dispute. The new Australian commitment to field troops in the Borneo territories and the statement of the former External Affairs Minister, Sir Garfield Barwick (later to be unceremoniously relieved of his post), that an attack on Australian troops would bring the USA into the picture under the ANZUS pact has taken Canberra farther aloug the road than it would have liked to go.

The USA is still maintaining her somewhat independent policy on Malaysia. But Britain has made significant breaches in Washington's approach to Indonesia. Continuing Indonesian military and political pressure on Malaysia has helped to force the USA to pare her aid to the bones and no future large-scale U.S. aid can be contemplated.

The position on the ground in May remains much as before. Indonesian guerrillas continue to intrude into the more inaccessible and less policed areas of Malaysian Borneo. Some are intercepted and shot, others escape; still others remain in pockets inside Malaysian territory. In spite of the fashion in Malaysia to belittle the troubled cease-fire negotiated by the U.S. Attorney-General, Mr Robert Kennedy, in January, it has exercised a somewhat moderating influence on the Indonesians.

The flurry of diplomatic activity is symptomatic of a general desire to prevent a polarization of forces in the area. If Indonesia continues to proceed along the road she has apparently taken, she would be reaching a point of no return. If Indonesian guerrilla activity in the Borneo territories is stepped up appreciably, it will force more and more of the Western Powers to take a British position on the Malaysia crisis.

The question therefore boils down to Indonesian objectives and terms for settlement. Indonesian leaders at present seem keen to retrace their steps in an Indonesian fashion, although their long-term objectives remain what they were: the dominance of South-East Asia. But even if Indonesia is given a helping hand by a third party, can President Soekarno tame the Indonesian Communist Party? The answer to this question is that only President Soekarno is capable of taking an unpopular decision since the political situation in Indonesia after him can at best be a subject of much speculation and uncertainty.

After his impressive victory in the Malayan general elections, Tengku Abdul Rahman has the freedom to arrive at a compromise settlement. A White Paper published in Kuala Lumpur contains a serious indictment of Indonesia; some of it must be dismissed as permissible propaganda but there seems little doubt that Indonesians had set about trying to subvert Malaysia with earnestness.

Malaysian leaders recognize that even if the two countries are friends again, Indonesian ideological subversion directed at the Malays will continue. But the problem facing them is whether they are to reconcile themselves to living in hostility with their big neighbour with all the heartbreaking problems it entails or, if there is a chance for a temporary settlement, should they grasp it in spite of the risks involved.

The Malaysia crisis is largely of Indonesia's making and Malaysia is, in many ways, an aggrieved party, as Kuala Lumpur continuously asserts. But the fund of bitterness building up in the two countries will do neither Malaysia nor Indonesia any good. And the greater the intensity of confrontation, the more will it show up Kuala Lumpur's dependence on Britain, besides posing the inevitable question of British willingness to bear the mounting costs of defending Malaysia for an indefinite period.

It would, however, be in Indonesia's own interest to arrive at a settlement without waiting for overtures from the Tengku. Technically, the point at issue between the two countries is Malaysia's insistence that Indonesian guerrillas leave the Borneo territories before talks on a political settlement can begin, while Indonesia demands that the latter precede the former.

Politicians in South-East Asia enjoy an enviable freedom of changing their minds overnight—without too many questions being asked. Although the Malaysia crisis might take a long time to be unscrambled, the process can be set into motion with amazing rapidity. The Maphilindo agreement between Malaysia, the Philippines and Indonesia remains a handy instrument for formalizing a temporary settlement. And the Philippines is more than willing to act as the master of ceremonies.

24

An inkling into the genesis of the Malaysia-Indonesia crisis can be had from a document published by Kuala Lumpur. It is an English translation of the proceedings of two plenary meetings held in 1945 of the Investigating Committee for the Preparation of Indonesia's Independence.

The committee resolved that "the territory of Free Indonesia will include the former Dutch East Indies with the addition of Malaya, North Borneo, Papua, Timor and the adjacent islands". Dr Soekarno was an enthusiastic supporter of this resolution. Dr Hatta's voice of reason, warning against the dangers of new imperialism, was drowned.

Being pragmatists, Indonesian leaders have redefined their national boundaries over the years to limit them to the former Dutch East Indies. The long campaign over West

Irian made the commitment to their new concepts more complete because they were at pains to allay suspicions that they had further territorial ambitions.

The concept of Malaysia was first broached when Indonesia was submerged in her propaganda and military campaign over West Irian. Indonesians believe in fighting one major issue at a time and Malaysia was therefore given a secondary place in their scheme of things; Dr Subandrio went to the extent of giving it faint praise at the United Nations.

Once the campaign over West Irian was successfully concluded, Indonesians were free to take issue with Malaysia. Indonesian leaders had given up the idea of incorporating Malaya, as they had earlier of taking in the Philippines; both countries were originally included in Dr Soekarno's concept of a Pan-Indonesia. The British Borneo territories, however, were another matter. Indonesian leaders had apparently hoped that with ideological warfare, these territories would gradually come within Indonesia's sphere of influence, finally to form a part of the Indonesian State.

Britain, however, was quick to anticipate Indonesia's future moves. By broaching the concept of Malaysia, the British plan was to change a predictable sequence of events; Britain's inspiration for Malaysia's formation is not in doubt although it was Tengku Abdul Rahman who made the proposal in May, 1961. London's primary interest in it was to rescue the British Borneo territories from Indonesia while for Malaya the concept's main attraction was that it solved the problem of Singapore's integration presented by its Chinese population. In commending Malaysia to the people of the Borneo territories, British officials made no secret of the fact that they were delivering them out of the "lion's jaws". Britain's role, as far as her traditional representation as the lion is concerned, was here reversed.

Indonesian leaders in consequence felt cheated and their particular animosity to Britain dates from this period. While Indonesians were exercising their minds in private over the question of "avenging British calumny", events in the tiny Sultanate of Brunei offered the ideal opportunity. The motivations of the Brunei revolt of December, 1962, were primarily internal but they tied up excellently with Indonesia's objectives. Mr Azahari and his Rakyat Party were Indonesian-oriented; dedicated Communists in the other Borneo territories were utilized to spread the revolt over all the three territories.

Mr Azahari is now a disliked man in Djakarta because Indonesia can never forgive him for having failed in pulling off the revolt. Had it succeeded, Indonesia could have given recognition to his "Government", thus puncturing the Malaysia concept. Because the revolt failed, the next best thing for Indonesia was to utilize it for propaganda purposes. A clandestine radio station was set up and an official status given to Mr Azahari's representative in Djakarta. The failure of the revolt also won for Indonesia a valuable ally in the Philippines.

The die was thus cast for much that was to follow, until President Macapagal, in an act of true statesmanship, propounded the Maphilindo scheme. Indonesia's dominant role in Maphilindo was assured and explicitly stated by the Philippines. This was accepted by Indonesia at the first three-nation summit in Manila last year; the fact that President Soekarno threw away this tailor-made plan to spread and consolidate his influence in the area for the dangerous and uncertain fruits of confrontation will rank as his biggest failure in a chequered political career.

A host of other factors greatly complicate the dispute over Malaysia. There are basic causes of conflict between Malaya (now Malaysia) and Indonesia. Indonesian political development has been such that it places a premium on revolution as against evolution. President Soekarno has sedulously cultivated the cult of Indonesian superiority, making it flow from the country having won its freedom through an armed struggle. And in solving Indonesia's Herculean problem of integration, he used the cement of extreme nationalism which is indistinguishable from chauvinism.

The West Irian episode provided Indonesia with substantial hardware from the Soviet Union. Indonesia is far from being a first-rate military power, but in terms of the capacities her neighbours possessed (and possess), the new acquisition of strength encouraged President Soekarno to flex his muscles and gave some substance to the Indonesian desire to dominate South-East Asia.

Malaya's political development, on the other hand, has been very subdued. Malaya's independence was not so much an achievement of Malayan leaders as an act of statesmanship on Britain's part. The structure of the feudal Sultans was retained in free Malaya; although their political powers were taken away, they were made the central arch in the edifice of Malays' political dominance. British interests in Malaya continued to predominate and the 30-year defence treaty signed with London dramatized the new State's dependence on Britain.

In spite of the great disparity between the two countries, Indonesian leaders were prepared to put up with Malaya as long as she acknowledged them as their political and spiritual mentors and treated them with due deference. This was not such an unwelcome prospect as it would seem. The Malays' political horizon was seriously limited by the inter-racial character of their country. The Chinese, comprising around 40% of the population, were the biggest non-European entrepreneurs; the Malays were, by and large, poor and ill-equipped to meet the Chinese challenge.

Indonesia, with her population of over 80 million Malays, was a source of much comfort to the Malays of Malaya and a widespread feeling among them was to seek very close ties, formalized if possible, with Indonesia. The Pan-Malayan Islamic Party, the only Opposition party to control any State Government in Malaya, is an exemplifica-ation of these feelings.

The Malaysia concept came as a rude shock to Indonesians because their pupils—as they considered the Malayan leaders—were not merely backing a British "plot" to deprive them of pieces of valuable territory but were also planning to benefit at their expense. This was seen as a piece of effrontery and went to create the bitter fruits of confrontation.

Malaysia touched another very sensitive spot of Indonesia. Against the background of island revolts that have continued to plague Djakarta, the new concept was seen as a diabolical plot to perpetuate British military presence around Indonesia. The Sumatra rebellion of 1957-58 and the encouragement it received from some of the Western Powers are strongly imprinted on the minds of Indonesian leaders. And a continuing British presence in the vicinity, it was felt in Djakarta, would provide Western Powers with an ideal opportunity to encourage revolts at a time of their choosing.

The Indonesians have used all the arguments they could muster to try to stem Malaysia. Apart from the theory of imperialistic encirclement of Indonesia, they developed the intriguing thesis that Malaysia's formation would only provide a stepping stone to Communism to invade the island nations of South-East Asia—a Chinese Singapore spreading out its fangs of Communism. They have also suggested to a West trying to stem Chinese influence in the area that Malaysia's formation would only encourage the local Chinese, whose basic sympathies for the mainland Government of China are not in doubt, to consolidate their hold over the new Federation.

When these arguments did not convince the better part of the world, Indonesia launched guerrilla warfare. Her gamble to have Malaysia undone through a United Nations investigation failed last year and she preferred to intensify her confrontation policy rather than accept Malaysia.

It is true that the people of the two former British territories of Sarawak and Sabah (North Borneo)—the British protectorate of Brunei chose to stay out of Malaysia for its own reasons—were apolitical. Organized political opinion, such as it was, particularly in Sarawak, was largely against Malaysia. This was because the Communists opposed the concept and the indigenous peoples feared Malayan domination.

The British played an indispensable part in throwing their considerable political influence behind Malaysia. But for this role and subsequent Malayan efforts to woo the local leaders, the new Federation would not have come about. However, the fact remains that a majority of the people of the two territories were eventually persuaded to see the benefits of Malaysia. Indonesians continue to challenge the process that brought this about.

The Malaysia-Indonesia crisis is, essentially, a conflict between an extreme form of nationalism and the efforts of a semi-feudal heterogeneous nation to find its place in the tempestuous world of South-East Asia. Around this central fact are enmeshed many interacting national and international factors.

With the astuteness the highest echelons of Indonesian leadership is capable of, Djakarta has calculated to a fine point its own importance in the East-West struggle in the area. With a population of over 100 million and a string of potentially rich islands stretching over a vast and vital strategic area, Indonesia has occupied a central position in the USA's Pacific Area plans.

U.S. tolerance and understanding of the frequent aberrations of Indonesian nationalism have stemmed from this basic American concern with Indonesia's strategic importance. Americans have also been impressed by the vitality of the people and the many attractive features Indonesian nationalism includes. Their hearty endorsement of the Maphilindo concept underlined this desire to encourage the great emotional base for Malay unity which can only help in stemming Chinese influence.

In spite of the hardware provided by the Soviet Union, Russian presence in Indonesia has never had a dramatic impact. As long as the Soviet Union was the undisputed Communist Power, Djakarta paid her due deference. With the Sino-Soviet conflict exploding on the world stage, Indonesians were quick to seize the opportunity to reorient their thinking and favours. According to a story related in Djakarta's diplomatic world with relish, the U.S. Ambassador is reported to have told his Soviet counterpart after a snub administered by President Soekarno to a high visiting Russian dignitary: "Mr Ambassador, not only are they playing the East against the West but the East against the East".

Indonesians have a basic prejudice against the Chinese, flowing from the long dominance of Chinese traders in the rural areas and their opulence in the cities. The anti-Chinese riots of last year were an example of this prejudice as also the earlier period of bedevilled relations between Djakarta and Peking over the question of Chinese traders.

Peking, however, chose to turn a blind eye to the anti-Chinese riots in order to continue its wooing of Indonesia. China's strongest base is the growing Indonesian Communist Party which is now dominated by the pro-Peking wing. And in the existing circumstances of Indonesia, all the vague but catchy jingoist slogans popularized by the apparatus of the Indonesian State are readily susceptible to Communist, particularly Chinese, exploitation.

Malaysia impinges on Indonesia's relations with these three Powers. The USA has been increasingly disillusioned by the pattern of recent events; in view of her present preoccupation with the Indo-China States and the polarization taking place there between the pro- and anti-Communist forces, American patience with Indonesia is beginning to be exhausted. U.S. aid has almost been stopped and earlier plans to provide substantial funds for Indonesian development have been put away.

Both China and the Soviet Union have formally supported Indonesia on the Malaysia dispute. China's support has been lacking in warmth, perhaps because there is a substantial Chinese population in Malaysia. But the Chinese policy is to continue to exploit the favourable circumstances of Indonesia while keeping her presence there as unobtrusive as possible.

Although the Soviet Union's present interests would seem to lie more in the direction of Maphilindo in terms of keeping Chinese influence at bay, she can hardly do less than reiterate her support to Indonesia. Russian supply of new weapons for Indonesia's confrontation policy and a new enthusiastic endorsement of Djakarta's position will do their bit to bolster the Soviet image in Indonesia. A period of increased Indonesian cordiality towards Russia is indicated, also because the Malaysia issue can figure in the United Nations where Djakarta will have to rely heavily on Soviet support.

Indonesian leaders seem convinced that the main hindrance to their Big Power ambitions is Britain's military power in South-East Asia. Djakarta has left severely alone the fact of America's greater power in the area because it benefits from the counterbalancing effects of the American presence on the Chinese. During the entire period of confrontation, Djakarta has concentrated its propaganda on seeking to remove British military presence from the area. It is, therefore, all the more ironical that Indonesia should have given short shrift to the Maphilindo project which foreshadowed a gradual replacement of the European Powers through regional defence arrangements.

Although Indonesian leaders are clear about their long-term objectives of being *the* Power in South-East Asia, their short-term policies are full of contradictions. Largely, these flow from the basic instability of the Indonesian State. President Soekarno's great contribution has been the integration of his fantastically varied country and in giving the ordinary Indonesian a sense of dignity. But he has failed to give his country a stable political structure, relying rather on his own charismatic appeal and the balancing of the PKI with the anti-Communist Armed Forces.

The problems presented by the disappearance of the balancing factor are so immense that they can only form the subject of speculation. It is also a universally recognized axiom that President Soekarno has no patience for economic planning. He has consistently made economic policies subservient to political objectives. Two dramatic instances have been his launching a trade boycott of Malaysia without adequate preparation and his willingness to sacrifice prospects of substantial foreign aid, a sorely needed commodity, for the dubious glories of confronting Malaysia. Economic instability has in consequence been exacerbated.

The Indonesian nation, on the other hand, is being continually fed on jingoism and there have been times during the long period of confrontation when the hands of the Indonesian leaders have been forced by the officially inspired euphoria on the Malaysia dispute. The PKI naturally throws its full weight behind nullifying any move for accommodation with Malaysia. Also, the Indonesian leaders' susceptibility to their own propaganda is having an increasingly limiting effect on their horizons.

The time has, however, arrived when Indonesia's actions are in danger of crowding out her long-term objective of playing a dominant role in the area. The only sensible alternative to continuing military confrontation is to adapt the concept to a purely ideological campaign and to revive the Maphilindo project. The three-nation Tokyo summit in June proved that President Soekarno was either unable or unwilling to give a chance to the proposed Afro-Asian Conciliation Commission to start work. If he continues to maintain this position, he will not only risk losing Filipino friendship but will also consign his country and South-East Asia to a new and dangerous phase of instability.

Malaysia is at the receiving end of much that happens today in relation to the dispute. While Indonesian confrontation has given the new Federation greater unity, it remains a jigsaw puzzle. Confrontation has not resolved the basic distrust between Malays and Chinese; Indians play a secondary role in the inter-racial suspicions. Indonesians are well aware of this as also the fact that over 60% of Malays are of Indonesian stock. They are utilizing the suspicions Malays have of the Chinese by continual propaganda blasts at Mr Lee Kuan Yew's Chinese State Government and the alleged hardships Malays suffer at its hands. It is also an indication of the strength of Malays' suspicions that; in spite of all the bitter fruits of confrontation, the Pan-Malayan Islamic Party retained its hold over the State of Kelantan in the recent Malayan elections.

Malaysia's defensive posture in relation to Indonesia does not flow entirely from its small size and lack of military resources and consequent dependence on a European Power. The inter-racial character has a very strong bearing on the dispute. Although Malaysian leaders are becoming increasingly resigned to a long period of strife with Indonesia, they have still fully to grasp all the hardships it will entail for their country.

Malaysia is an affluent country but its affluence largely comes from the export of the two primary products—rubber and tin—which are proverbially susceptible to changing (usually falling) world prices. Malaysia's formation means that the Federal Government will have to make increasing development outlays in the Borneo territories while intensifying rural development in Malaya. Spectacular jumps in the Malaysian Defence Budget are the inevitable result of Indonesia's continuing confrontation. They are a new burden on the national exchequer. Singapore, however, has largely weathered the storm created by Indonesia's trade boycott.

Peace therefore is a very welcome prospect for Malaysia although there are hotheads in Kuala Lumpur trying to emulate the Indonesian brand of nationalism by proposing various measures, including the encouragement of dissident tendencies in Sumatra, an island traditionally at odds with the Javanese-dominated Central Government and more conservative in political outlook. Confrontation has, besides, given the Malaysian Chinese the opportunity to oppose Maphilindo vigorously. Will peace arrive? The answer to this question largely depends upon Indonesia. President Soekarno does not have much time to give the answer.

25

A confrontation between the Malays and Chinese had to take place. It came sooner than expected, in the form of racial violence in Singapore in July claiming over 20 lives. Inevitably, this aberration throws up vital issues affecting the future of the new Federation and an estimated 12 million overseas Chinese in South-East Asia.

Except in Malaysia, in which they form the largest single racial block, the problems overseas Chinese face in a sprawling, unsettled South-East Asia are similar. Through industriousness and an almost uncanny knack of amassing wealth, they have prospered in spite of their small numbers. They are the most inbred of racial minorities and rarely mix, except at superficial social and business levels.

In one country after another, overseas Chinese have had to pay for their racial exclusiveness and prosperity. As nationalism took hold of the emerging nations, discriminatory laws were passed against them. But the Chinese adjusted themselves to circumstances and survived in spite of them. They changed their names, as in Indonesia and Thailand; married local women even though they had wives in China, to acquire local business status, like in Burma and Cambodia; renounced their Chinese nationality (for form's sake), for instance in Indonesia, to acquire indigenous citizenship. When these expedients failed, the divergence between discriminatory laws and reality was often so great that they could easily earn their living and more under cover.

Sometimes, popular resentment against Chinese opulence in the midst of indigenous poverty spilled over in racial violence, as happened in Indonesia last year. The Chinese take these storms with a stoic calm and continue from where they had left off. South-East Asian Governments have tolerated their Chinese minorities with varying degrees of disfavour.

Apart from the social, economic and racial problems overseas Chinese pose in all of South-East Asia, the political implications of their descent from the Communist rulers of modern China have been a source of constant worry to many Governments. In countries where anti-Communist Governments are in power, as in the Philippines and Thailand, the local Chinese have given their formal allegiance to the Formosan regime. But two suspicions about overseas Chinese have remained. Can they subordinate their racial pride to the national interests of their adopted countries? Can they change their basic attachment to mainland China, transcending as it does the ideological and political bent of the ruling power in Peking?

South-East Asian Governments have, in the ultimate analysis, drawn comfort from the fact that their Chinese minorities are in controllable numbers. This comfort is denied the Malays of Malaysia who are, in actual fact, a minority compared to the strength of the Chinese population. The old Malayan Constitution gave Malays political dominance through special rights and privileges, through making Islam the State religion and through the superstructure of Sultans who were made the religious guardians of the country. Besides, citizenship laws were made selective and discriminatory to depress the Chinese vote.

These arrangements have worked to a limited extent in Malaya. Under a veneer of Malay political dominance, the Chinese have, however, continued to prosper while the Government's many schemes for correcting the imbalance between Malay poverty and Chinese prosperity have had little impact, benefiting only a minority among the Malays. The older generation of the Chinese have been largely content with this scheme of things.

Malaysia's formation in September last year introduced a startling factor in the shape of Singapore. In Malaya, except during phases of the 12-year Emergency, the Chinese largely presented a mild front and paid lip service to the concept of Malaya being the particular homeland of Malays.

But Singapore was a different thing altogether. The island's overwhelming Chinese population gave them confidence about their future and the brand of radical politics Singapore bred produced a different type of Chinese leader.

A crisis in Malay-Chinese relations was inevitable as new generations of local-born Chinese were reaching voting age, gradually to erode some of the artificial barriers of the Constitution. With Singapore's integration into Malaysia and the racial overtones of Indonesian propaganda, the crisis point was advanced by several decades.

Only a Lee Kuan Yew, with his razor-sharp mind and ruthless tactics, could have brought Singapore into Malaysia by outmanoeuvring the Communists at their own game. But even as he went about the process of breaking the back of Communist power, he aroused suspicions in many Malay minds. Although Chinese votes had brought him to power in Singapore, Mr Lee sought to give an inter-racial tinge to his People's Action Party and dramatically illustrated the success of his strategy by winning a sizable proportion of Malay votes in Singapore's elections last year. Malay suspicions reached a fever pitch at this stage; many unprintable things were said about Mr Lee as Malay leaders saw visions of a Lee Kuan Yew seeking to destroy their highly prized political privileges through a Chinese-dominated inter-racial pan-Malayan party.

Mr Lee's string of heady successes, in Singapore's "referendum", in the island's general elections and in momentarily subduing Communists, induced him to overplay his hand early this year. In spite of specific assurances to the contrary, the People's Action Party decided to contest Malaya's general elections in April. Malay leaders took this as an act of deliberate poaching which gave substance to their nightmares of Mr Lee as a potential ruler of Malaysia. The PAP's crushing defeat in Malaya, however, brought little comfort to the United Malays National Organization although it did to the Chinese partner in the Alliance, the Malayan Chinese Association.

Mr Lee showed his hand too clearly for UMNO leaders' liking and they set about confronting the Singapore Prime Minister on his home ground through agitating for special privileges for Malays residing on the island. The tragedy of it was that even as they went about the task of paying back Mr Lee in his own coin, to exorcize the ghost of an indigenous Chinese threat to their own nationhood, they paid no heed to the wider political implications of their racial agitation. While Mr Lee had, in many ways, invited this trouble, the Malay wing of the Central Government showed a conspicuous lack of foresight in failing to curb a tremendously explosive agitation, in spite of repeated warnings by the Singapore Administration.

The Singapore riots' link with the problem of overseas Chinese is in the person of its Prime Minister. Mr. Lee is a young politician schooled in Communist methods of acquiring power and has much drive and will power. He has made it abundantly clear in words and action (he is a voluble speaker in English, Malay and several dialects of Chinese) that Singapore's area is too small to contain his ambition. Although his party was badly mauled in the Malayan elections, it seems to be a question of time before he will claim the allegiance of a majority of Chinese in Malaya. He has a little under five years in which to vary his tactics to gather Chinese votes in the peninsula. His insistence on the Chinese right to live in equality—an argument he has been propounding before and during the riots—has already won him the esteem of many Chinese.

Mr Lee's race confines him to the attainable ambition of leadership of Malaysian Chinese. He himself expressed the view some time ago that there cannot be a Chinese

Prime Minister of Malaysia for at least 20 years. And all indications suggest that he is anticipating his winning over the allegiance of a majority of Malaysian Chinese by projecting himself in the future role of leader of all overseas Chinese.

Such a role would be commensurate with his ambitions and could change the concept of the place of overseas Chinese in South-East Asia. So far, overseas Chinese have often had to pay lip service to Formosa while retaining basic sympathy for the growing power and prestige of mainland China. If Mr Lee succeeds in attaining his objectives, he could provide a third way for overseas Chinese, securing in the bargain a potent political instrument of power in the region.

Mr Lee seems to be etching this role for himself by planting firmly the flag of a new Malaysian Chinese nationalism while at the same time running up another flag in harsh opposition to Maphilindo. Opposition to the latter concept—an expression of Malay nationalism which would work against the interests of overseas Chinese and thus of Peking, to which they are readily susceptible—can only bring comfort to the Chinese of Indonesia and the Philippines, too small in numbers to voice effective protest.

Mr Lee has already formulated a broad basis for a new Chinese nationalism during the riots and the Malay agitation preceding it, inviting the accusation from Malay leaders of seeking to create an Israel in Singapore. The Chinese, he says, are entitled to a free and full life in a country which calls itself democratic and while Malay poverty should be alleviated, the Chinese should not be levelled down. The concept is not new or unique, but its projection is. Singapore's Chinese majority and the island's key position in Malaysia give Mr Lee the opportunity of speaking up on Chinese political rights; he seems to have calculated the reprisals he can invite in the process.

The Singapore Prime Minister's ambitions are thus completely opposed to the aims of the Malay-dominated Central Government, unlike during the agitation against Malaysia when the immediate objectives of the two parties coincided. How far Mr Lee will agree to compromise an objective he seems to have set his heart upon in order to keep Malaysia intact remains to be seen. Malaysia is as vital to his objectives as it is to those of the Malays, although for very different reasons. The next few months will provide another fascinating chapter in the history of a turbulent island.

26

There are many missing pieces in a jigsaw puzzle Kuala Lumpur is trying to decipher. But if the puzzle answers to Malaysian beliefs, it will have shattering implications for peace in the region and the world.

Although Malaysian leaders tend to treat their hypothesis as a proven fact, it is no more than an assumption for the present. The evidence in Kuala Lumpur's possession, however, is impressive enough to merit study. Briefly, the Malaysian thesis is that China is using the Indonesian Communist Party and the remnants of the anti-Malayan Communist uprising to start an armed rebellion covering Southern Thailand, Malaya, Singapore and the Borneo island.

There is first of all a secret directive of the underground Communist Party of Malaya of September, 1963, obtained from a captured party member. Malaysian officials say there can be no doubt about its authenticity. The directive calls upon the people of the Malaysian Borneo territories, Brunei and Malaya to undertake an armed struggle, along with peaceful measures, to undo Malaysia and "free" Malaya and the Borneo territories.

A close liaison between the Malayan Communist Party and the PKI is entirely plausible. Malayan Communists naturally incline to Peking, in view of their racial affiliations. Since the PKI is patronized by the Chinese and is a powerful next-door neighbour of the MCP, it would give whatever succour it could to the latter.

The PKI has been loud in protesting against Malaysia and has frowned upon any move for a rapprochement. One of the central factors in a possible peaceful settlement of the Malaysia-Indonesia crisis is: Can President Soekarno afford to offend the PKI? The Indonesian Communists' main base is in overpopulated Java but new indications suggest that they are building up strength in Indonesian Borneo under the guise of sending National Front volunteers to "crush" Malaysia.

Communist infiltration of the Malaysian Borneo territories, particularly Sarawak, has been a historical problem. After plans to set up Malaysia were announced, the British have had an arduous job keeping the Communists under control. The Brunei revolt of December, 1962, brought out the Sarawak Communists in an open armed action; almost entirely Chinese in composition, they were put down with the help of various stringent measures, including deportation to China. Over the past several months, however, reports have been flowing in of Chinese youths disappearing from their homes. Present estimates are that over 2,000 Sarawak Chinese Communists and sympathizers have crossed the border into Indonesian Borneo.

The rather archaic and inadequate name given to the Sarawak Communist Party is Clandestine Communist Organization. British reports say that the CCO is a self-contained unit. Many Malaysians disagree with this assessment because of the pressures operating on the CCO from the PKI in Borneo and the MCP in Singapore.

In the north, the joint Malayan-Thai operations against the remaining 500 Communist guerrillas left over from the 12-year Emergency were called off early last year. Kuala Lumpur officials explain this rather surprising decision by saying that the guerrillas had ceased to be a military threat. These hard-core Communists along the Northern Malaya-Thai border have therefore been left to their own devices for over a year.

Malaysian reports say that the Communist leaders have been experiencing difficulty in keeping up the morale of this force. Some of them have been allowed to go home, others have been put to learning Malay. Communist Malay leaders have been utilized to stir up irredentist tendencies in Southern Thailand.

One of the traditional planks of the opposition Pan-Malayan Islamic Party is the merger of the Southern Muslim provinces of Thailand into Malaya. This has embarrassed the Tengku Abdul Rahman Government as much as it has caused concern to the Thais. Unconfirmed reports have said that arms were being supplied to the border guerrillas from Indonesian sources. No evidence has been produced to substantiate these reports which have, however, persuaded the Thai Government to send troops to its southern border.

Malaysian sources refuse to divulge the evidence they have to support their belief that some of the top Communist guerrillas from the border region are now in Peking receiving instructions. Among those believed to be in China is the foremost Malayan Communist leader, Chin Peng. Malaysians further believe that the MCP is now looking to China for material support; the party did not receive such support during the 12-year guerrilla war in Malaya.

There are two other interesting pieces of evidence from Malaya. About 50 Chinese middle school students disappeared from an area of Johore State in May. Some parents are reported to have received letters from their sons bearing Indonesian postmarks. A few hundred such students are reported to have left Malaya for Indonesia.

It has also been officially confirmed that in an area of Pahang State in Malaya, a number of Malay Communist guerrillas who had surrendered, and were later rehabilitated, have left their settlements for an unknown destination.

It is the Malaysian belief that all these activities indicate a Chinese-supported Communist plan to start an armed revolt on two major fronts: Borneo and North Malaya. Malaysians fear that the few thousand Chinese who have gone to Indonesia from Sarawak and Malaya will be trained and indoctrinated before being sent back to start a South Vietnam type of guerrilla war.

The present objectives of the PKI and President Soekarno in "crushing" Malaysia coincide. Indonesian Communists are naturally trying to use the anti-Malaysia campaign for their own ends. However, it cannot yet be said with any degree of assurance that the PKI is receiving active Chinese support for the specific aim of capturing the Borneo island for Communism.

The back of the 12-year guerrilla war in Malaya was broken by one crucial factor. An overwhelming number of guerrillas were Chinese and the inter-racial factors operating in the country made it possible to isolate the guerrilla war as a Chinese phenomenon. Malaysians believe that the new armed uprising the Communists are planning will be a Sino-Malay operation. In view of the Malay base the PKI has in Indonesia and efforts being made to train Malay guerrillas in Indonesian Borneo and along the Northern Malayan border, an inter-racial Communist offensive is within the realm of possibility.

The weakest link in the chain of Malaysian arguments, however, is that Kuala Lumpur believes, rather too readily, that President Soekarno is a virtual prisoner in PKI's hands. The growing strength of the PKI in Indonesia restricts the Indonesian Government's freedom in undertaking major policy decisions which go contrary to Communist objectives. President Soekarno's problems are further bedevilled by the state of the nation's economy. But it is a far cry to suggest that he has already capitulated to the Communists.

The danger in the situation is that if the chaotic conditions of Indonesia continue for long, the main beneficiary would be the PKI. The peculiar amalgam of Indonesian instability and radicalism and its present anti-Malaysia campaign could tie up excellently with Chinese objectives of subsequently exploiting Malaysia's many contradictions for a Communist-inspired guerrilla war.

A Chinese decision to utilize the explosive potentialities of the Malaysia-Indonesia crisis will, however, depend upon the success of its aims in the Indo-China States. The frightening prospect is that Peking could, with very little effort, start a conflagration in the Malayan peninsula. Malaysians go a step further in saying that China has already decided to set fire to the inviting tinder of Malaysian-Indonesian differences to submerge Malaya in a more horrifying guerrilla war than it has lived through.

27

The sleepy town of Labis of 5,000 people on the trunk road from Kuala Lumpur to Singapore is swarming with armoured cars and military and police officers and men as a result of the Indonesians' airdrop of some 30 people eight miles from there on September 2.

As I drove into Labis around noon three days after the Indonesian landings, a 24-hour curfew was imposed to enable the Army to flush out the remaining members of the Indonesian party. British Gurkha and New Zealand troops were planning to shell the area, a new land development scheme surrounded by rubber plantations and thick jungle, used by Indonesians for the airdrop of men and supplies.

Earlier in the morning a 19-year-old Malaysian Chinese girl was led into the Labis police station in tears. She had taken a ride in a timber lorry and was detected at a police check-point. She was one of the two girls airdropped by Indonesians and had apparently intended to give herself up. She carried a bundle of clothes, a Malaysian identity card (which every resident in the country has to have) and was apparently among the few hundred young Chinese who had disappeared from their homes in Johore in May.

In the Labis police station I met an Indonesian commando airdropped on September 2. Tobitabran was sitting in the police lock-up in handcuffs. A diffident man with a sparse beard, he said he came from Djakarta where his parents were still living. He said he had received about three years' training in the commando unit of the Indonesian Air Force and was a private. When I asked him why he had participated in the dangerous venture, he replied: "I was ordered to come here to liberate the people of Malaya from the British. Now I am disillusioned. "Police officers described Tobitabran as a "very co-operative" prisoner.

In the compound of the Labis police station, which is serving as headquarters for the entire operations, I saw parachutes, ammunition, steel helmets and other Army equipment brought in by villagers from the scene of the Indonesian landings. Most of the articles were of American manufacture. Among the goods exhibited were American Army rations and Malaysian officials accompanying me made caustic comments about the use previous U.S. military aid to Indonesia was being put to.

Labis was one of the worst areas during the 12-year war with Communist guerrillas in Malaya. That seems to be the only valid reason why Indonesians selected the area to make their first air landings. It was a dark misty night when the landings were made and some Malaysian officials presume that the Indonesians mistook the clearing for a helicopter field in the adjoining jungle used by the British for anti-guerrilla operations during the previous Emergency.

Officials in Labis are particularly pleased with the reaction of the local people. They are not only eager to report new faces in their settlements but also willingly serve as guides to the Army in the operations. Vigilante corps had been formed in the area only a few weeks earlier, after the Indonesians' Pontian seaborne landings. Members of vigilante corps in the area were the first to spot the aircraft and the landings and they got the manager of a nearby rubber estate to telephone the police in the early hours of the morning of September 2.

Of the party of Indonesians and Malaysians airdropped, four have been killed and eight captured. The Gurkhas and New Zealanders have now moved in to relieve the Malaysian battalion which was required to cope with the Singapore riots.

28

Malaysia's jazzy new Parliament House in Kuala Lumpur lends an air of unreality to the prevailing crisis in the country. It stands on a hill commanding a splendid view of the capital. Parts of Kuala Lumpur are almost rustic in their charm and appearance and the neatly ordered old houses rarely mix with the ultramodern expressions of national pride. Neither give an indication of crisis. Only the chaotic traffic in the city, going round in circles because of a proliferation of one-way streets, gives evidence of the pulse-beat of a capital enmeshed in a crisis.

It has long been the wont of Malayan leaders to present situations in black and white. Public discussion of the nuances of a problem is almost unheard of. The new Emergency, proclaimed by the Paramount Ruler in September and approved by Parliament after a one-day debate, can only accentuate this trend. The crisis is presented to the people as a fight on two fronts: against a President Soekarno virtually a prisoner in Communist hands and against local Communists who have never reconciled themselves to their defeat during the 12-year Emergency.

Although it is comforting to make such a tidy packet of the country's prevailing troubles, few are misled by the official version, which is incomplete. There have, of course, been the usual expressions of loyalty and support. A trade union in Singapore has announced that it would deprive its members of 15 minutes of their lunch break. Other unions have not been wanting in making strident condemnations of Indonesian actions. But the most uncomfortable aspects of the crisis are too many and too close to be swept away under the carpet.

The Parliament debate on the Emergency threw up one aspect of the internal crisis. Singapore's Barisan Socialist Party bluntly opposed the measure, casting a prediction of doom on Malaysia. Two Malayan Opposition parties—the Pan-Malayan Islamic Party and the Socialist Front—felt it expedient to support the Emergency with reservations. But they took the opportunity to ask the Government to sue for peace with Indonesia.

That the two main Opposition parties in Malaya should ask the Government to make peaceful overtures to Indonesia at a time when the country is threatened by continuing border incursions in Borneo and Indonesian infiltration into the mainland is a reflection of the people's divided loyalties. It is, indeed, ironical that a party of the extreme Right like the PMIP, standing for the union of the Malay race across four countries, should find itself siding with Chinese Communist sympathizers who are influenced by Indonesia's radical politics and China's support for Djakarta.

The Emergency debate also produced some undertones. Singapore's People's Action Party, which distinguishes itself from the other opposition parties in the Malaysian Parliament by calling itself a responsible opposition, fully supported the Emergency. At the same time, its spokesman gave a warning against undue Central interference with States' rights. This warning was an expression of a Chinese Singapore's fears of the Malay-dominated Central Government.

These two internal problems have merged during the present crisis. There is, on one hand, distrust between the two main races, as the Singapore riots clearly indicated. Secondly, mutual suspicions between Mr Lee Kuan Yew's PAP and the United Malays National Organization have far from ended. A dialogue is continuing between Singapore and Kuala Lumpur on these two issues.

The Singapore riots have forced Malay and Chinese leaders to continue their arguments in a lower key. The Malaysian Prime Minister has applied the balm of his mild, convivial personality during visits to Singapore. Malaya's Rural and Industrial Development Authority (RIDA) will enter the island to give Malays special benefits in housing and welfare services. This Central effort to soothe Malay fears of the Chinese State Government could provide temporary relief. However, racial animosities, once aroused, cannot disappear overnight, with Indonesian and Communist propaganda seeking to instigate new race riots and Mr Lee Kuan Yew attempting to fashion his future out of the present crisis.

There have been demands from UMNO branches in Malaya that Mr Lee should be redesignated Chief Minister and other demands that he should be replaced. Malays also complain, with some justification, that Singapore's radio and television networks are dominated by Mr Lee's activities and views, to the exclusion of other legitimate interests.

A British newspaper's unjustified comparison between the Tengku's policies towards the Chinese and Sir Roy Welensky's towards the non-White in the former Central African Federation aroused a storm of protest from Malays. A delegation of the youth wing of UMNO made a formal protest to the British High Commissioner in Kuala Lumpur, Lord Head, who is reported to have pointed out that freedom of the Press had different connotations in Britain and Malaysia.

The British newspaper's unsavoury comparison immediately led to accusations that since the comment appeared immediately after Mr Lee Kuan Yew's London visit, dominated by Press and television interviews, it was inspired by him. A propaganda campaign against the few Malays associated with Mr Lee in prominent posts has also been mounted. Some foreign correspondents based in Singapore have come under heavy fire from Malay leaders for their reporting on the Singapore riots. These reports, generally critical of the role of some Malay leaders, were played back by Mr Lee's State Government.

Trivial as some of these incidents might appear to the outside world, they vividly reflect the internal strains Malaysia is undergoing. The Singapore Prime Minister's answer has been to declare publicly at every conceivable occasion that Malaysia can survive only through a non-racial approach. He calls the proportions in which the two main races are to be found in Malaysia a "built-in incentive" for non-racial politics. Singapore's radio and television networks carry exhortations along these lines. Kuala Lumpur's radio station, on the other hand, concentrates on warning the people against President Soekarno's actions.

Laudable as Mr Lee's exhortations are, they do not give the answer to the basic problems posed by the racial composition of Malaysia; nor, it must be said, do the present schemes of the Malay leaders. It is a gross oversimplification of problems to suggest that the Malaysian Chinese should be immediately given all the political rights the Malays possess. The economic disparity between the two races is so vastly in Chinese favour that a Chinese dominance in the political field as well could create conditions of civil war beside posing the problem of Peking's influence over the affairs of the country.

Malays say that their social and economic backwardness is a result of the colonial pattern of development which brought immigrant labour and kept Malays backward. The Chinese reply that it is not their fault that their ancestors were encouraged to migrate to what is now Malaysia. They add that their economic prosperity is the result of hard work. There is truth in assertions made on both sides but the past can hardly serve as a guide to the future, and broadside attacks on a "Malay Malaysia" being made by Mr Lee will not help in resolving the problem.

It must also be remembered that the Chinese in Malaysia enjoy a greater degree of freedom than overseas Chinese communities in any other State of South-East Asia. Rich Chinese in Singapore are, indeed, fearful that the prevailing atmosphere can harm their interests and it is an open secret that some of them have transferred their liquid assets to Hongkong and London.

Indonesia's confrontation policy has deprived Malaysia of the leisure in which to work out its race problems. The Chinese are demanding equal political rights, with Mr Lee acting as the symbol of their revolt. The Malays who outnumber the Chinese only when counted with the indigenous people of the Borneo States, are zealously nursing their special rights, based upon religion and race. The new Chinese mood can only encourage extremist tendencies among Malays, who fear that their vision of a genuine homeland bringing them prosperity and happiness could be destroyed by the consequences of Malaysia's formation.

Mr Lee's strength is that, in view of Indonesian pressures, responsible Malay leaders have to continue to exercise restraint over their extremist sections. Indonesian-operated rebel radio stations, meanwhile, broadcast virulent propaganda designed to arouse anti-Chinese feelings among Malays. Djakarta is at the same time attempting to coax the Chinese to rebel against Malaysia, with Peking lending a willing hand. For the moment, the racial cauldron is simmering but it could go on the boil again.

29

A Government White Paper, issued in Kuala Lumpur in October, traces the pattern of Indonesian subversion in the two Borneo States of Sabah and Sarawak, now comprising Eastern Malaysia, before and after the formation of the Federation in September last year.

The White Paper's main conclusion is that the Indonesians have failed in their objective of building up a local grassroot dissident movement in the Borneo States. They are, therefore, shifting their objective to one of creating "alarm and despondency" in Eastern Malaysia to force political concessions from the Federation.

This is by no means the most interesting aspect of the official document, which relies heavily on the testimony of more than 60 Indonesian guerrillas captured in the Borneo States. It is estimated that a total of eight Indonesian infantry and marine commando battalions and 12 units of irregular forces are spread along the Malaysian-Borneo borders. Units vary from 25 to 125 men.

A total of 214 incidents in the two Borneo States involving Indonesian terrorists are catalogued. The first incident occurred at Tebedu in Sarawak's First Division on April 12 last year in which a group estimated to be 30 strong, led by an Indonesian Army officer, attacked a security post, killed a member of the Security Forces and captured weapons and ammunition.

Many of the volunteers sent out in the early phase of Indonesia's military confrontation seem to have been expendable material. They were apparently pressed into joining the volunteer units, skimpingly trained in army camps in Indonesian Borneo and sent on their hazardous missions on the dictates of Djakarta's political requirements.

Receiving little local encouragement, the morale of the guerrillas declined rapidly in the inhospitable jungles of Borneo. Harassed by sickness, starvation and the Security Forces, a number of them preferred to surrender rather than die an unsung death.

About 1,000 Chinese youths belonging to Sarawak's underground Communist Party (in official jargon, the Clandestine Communist Organization) are believed to have crossed into Indonesian Borneo for training in subversion. Those captured among this group, however, gave an impression of Indonesian equivocation in associating them with the volunteer groups sent into Malaysia. Some of them were given Iban names and no exclusively Chinese volunteer units were formed.

The White Paper speculates that the Indonesian authorities probably felt that their help to Malaysian Chinese Communists would make their country unpopular with a majority of the Sarawak people. Also, in view of the Indonesian distrust of the Chinese, the authorities might not have wished to advertise their support for a Chinese movement.

In Sabah, the White Paper traces Indonesian subversion back to the setting up of an Indonesian Consulate in Jesseltion in January, 1962. The Consulate is alleged to have set out to assume control over nearly 20,000 Indonesian immigrant labour on plantations and in timber camps. Several Indonesian-inspired local subversive organizations were formed, apparently without much success, and a system of secret travel passes arranged for Indonesian couriers. One such pass was discovered in March inside a cake of soap aboard a barter trading vessel about to leave Tawau for Indonesia.

The White Paper links the intrusion of particular Indonesian volunteer groups with Djakarta's objective of extracting political concessions from Malaysia at the conference table. At least two volunteer groups, it says, were despatched after President Soekarno had declared a temporary ceasefire on January 23. Two days after the Manila three-nation summit meeting, a force of 70 was contacted in Sarawak and four military formations invaded the State within two weeks of the publication of the U.N. report on the Borneo territories and Malaysia's formation. With the approach of the three-nation summit meeting in Tokyo in June, determined incursions were made into Sarawak.

Following the failure of Indonesia's earlier objective of creating an internal movement of dissension, Djakarta is increasing the proportion of regular soldiers in the infiltrating units. In any event, Indonesia has now admitted that her nationals are in Malaysian Borneo as volunteers. A campaign was, in fact, launched in March to recruit volunteers from all parts of Indonesia to "crush" Malaysia. Although a total of 21 million are claimed to have been recruited, Kuala Lumpur's estimate is that only two million volunteers have actually been registered.

30

It was a particularly oppressive afternoon in Kuala Lumpur when the National Solidarity Week was launched in November. VIPs sat sweltering in the heat in the sports stadium, where the ceremony was held. Out in the bowl, Government employees and students stood in the sun holding aloft banners inscribed with *Berjaya*, a Malay word which has connotations of both success and victory.

The purpose of the Solidarity Week was to dramatize the need for unity in the face of Indonesian confrontation. Most of the people who had flocked to the stadium were treating the occasion as an outing, as people are in the habit of treating such ceremonies anywhere in the world. A long afternoon stretched out interminably as orations in Malay, Chinese and Tamil piled up. And it started raining while Tengku Abdul Rahman spoke. The bowl was soon half empty as people ran for cover.

Even as the strains of the peppy police band had died down, politicians resumed their discussions on Mr Lee Kuan Yew. Mr Lee has become a national preoccupation in Kuala Lumpur and the feelings he arouses are something approaching those Mr Khrushchev has aroused among the leaders of China. The parallel cannot be taken too far because Mr Lee is no Khrushchev and Malay leaders have little in common with those of China, but the depth of feeling in both instances is similar.

Optimists in Kuala Lumpur point out that progress has been achieved in bringing Malaya and Singapore nearer to each other's viewpoint since Malayan independence. Before Tengku Abdul Rahman formally broached the concept of Malaysia in 1961, the two Prime Ministers were hardly on speaking terms. But a year after Singapore became a part of Malaysia, tension between Kuala Lumpur and Singapore has reached frightening proportions. Recent efforts to paper over the cracks do not attempt to solve the basic causes of the deep division; they merely give a much-needed breathing space, and Mr Lee continues to exercise Malay minds in Kuala Lumpur.

Some differences between Kuala Lumpur and Singapore are natural and inevitable. Singapore is a closely-knit Chinese city State with a relatively accomplished working population. Entrepot trade and the insurance and banking facilities it has helped to establish have made the city prosperous. It is taken for granted that when Malaysian common market arrangements are implemented, the city's growing industries will benefit greatly because of the new duty-free market their products will enjoy within Malaysia.

Malaya, on the other hand, is largely an agricultural hinterland where Malays, counted with other "indigenous" people, are in a majority and enjoy special political privileges, with the Sultans acting as symbols of their position. Malay politicians have always had their suspicions of Singapore because of the city's radical politics and Chinese preponderance.

Adjustments between Malaya and Singapore would therefore have posed inevitable problems. But the twist given by two bouts of communal rioting in Singapore and

Mr Lee's personality and tactics have combined with the stresses produced by Indonesian confrontation to make Mr Lee the centre of Malay resentment.

The basic Malay fear about Mr Lee is that his efforts to win over the Chinese in Malaysia are but the first step towards attempting to become the country's Prime Minister. A Chinese Prime Minister for Malaysia is extremely unlikely in the foreseeable future, but Mr Lee has, for his own reasons, made no effort to assuage Malay fears on this point. Besides, he has seized upon the riots to claim equal political privileges for the Chinese in Malaysia.

Mr Lee's prolific public utterances are, for the most part, unexceptionable; their undertones and timing, however, serve as a nagging reminder to Malays to be on their guard. Also, Mr Lee holds periodic "councils of war" with a selective number of foreign correspondents often to pour derision on Malay leaders in Kuala Lumpur and utter dire warnings about the future. Inevitably, word about these meetings percolates to Kuala Lumpur.

The effect of Mr Lee's words and actions has been to fan Malay fears to an alarming extent. An immediate Malay reaction is to point out the great disparity between Malay poverty and Chinese prosperity. A survey carried out some time ago revealed that if all European assests in Malaya were distributed among the Malays, the Chinese would still be twice as rich. In Kuala Lumpur, one Malay leader put the position to me thus: "If Indonesia were to bomb Kuala Lumpur, who would lose? All these grand buildings belong to the Chinese; Malays own only a few acres of rubber." Another asked of me the rhetorical question: "If a referendum were to be held today on Malaysia, what would be its result?"

Many Malay leaders are more circumspect in propounding their views but they share, in varying degrees, a particular dislike for Mr Lee. It is the devout wish of all of them to see Mr Lee leave the State's Prime Ministership. They hopefully ask whether there are differences within the People's Action Party. Mr Lee's position, however, shows no sign of weakening, a fact which only increases Malay frustrations, particularly because of the unabashed Western admiration for Mr Lee. Besides, the Singapore Prime Minister's weakness for scoring points further exacerbates Malay feelings. For instance, the Malay Press has in the past made direct and vulgar attacks on Mr Lee; the latter's answer has been to translate these into English and distribute them widely, reserving his own strong comments on Malay leaders for private briefings.

Mr Lee's many tactical victories and the admiration he arouses in the West have placed Malay leaders on the defensive. They concede that he is running an efficient State Government but they point to the island's size, compared to Malaya's area. They say they could achieve similar efficiency in Malaya if they chose to follow Mr Lee's methods, but that they are wedded to democracy. Malay leaders in Kuala Lumpur are inclined to treat democracy as an albatross they carry around their necks, but for which they would perform miracles.

While all Malay leaders would be happy to see Mr Lee fade away from the political scene, their views on the best method of coping with him vary. This has produced stresses within the United Malays National Organization. Speculation about a power struggle in UMNO is dismissed by Malay leaders as an attempt by Singapore to "split" the Malays.

It is, however, true that younger elements are seeking a greater say in UMNO. Tun Abdul Razak's position as the next Prime Minister after the Tengku, now in his sixties, retires seems unassailable. Tun Razak would perhaps not be in the same position as the Tengku is to withstand extremist pressures although he is a sober and competent leader. It is no secret that Mr Lee does not particularly welcome the prospect of Tun Razak's accession to the country's highest office and the Tengku's Political Secretary has had to deny rumours about the Tun's alleged anti-Chinese inclinations.

During an extended visit to Malaya, Mr. Lee had political talks with the Tengku. He announced that they had resulted in a two-year moratorium; the People's Action Party agreed not to extend its branches in Malaya during the period. Mr Lee later explained that the moratorium did not compel UMNO to restrict its activities on the island. Yet plans announced by a Central Minister, who heads Singapore UMNO, to streamline the organization in the State drew the charge from the PAP that the agreement had been violated. The Tengku said his understanding with Mr Lee was that both sides should avoid communal issues during the present period of emergency.

What transpired between the Tengku and Mr Lee has been the subject of much controversy. According to reports prevalent in Kuala Lumpur, the Tengku did a lot of plain-speaking, pointing out the dangers of exciting racial feelings and the consequences they would have on Singapore's own future. Mr Lee seems to have been sufficiently concerned to offer a two-year understanding on a sensitive issue but the basis of this understanding, being private in nature, has led to charges and counter-charges.

Mr Lee's strength lies in the fact that he is in an unassailable position in Singapore and stands a fair chance of winning over the Chinese in Malaya. Malaysia's existence, however, is vital to his larger ambitions and there are obvious dangers in driving Malays to the point of their seeking desperate remedies. If Malays had to choose between political domination by the Chinese and union with Indonesia, they would prefer the latter.

Speculation about Singapore's possible cession from Malaysia was given a shot in the arm some time ago by the Central Finance Minister, Mr Tan Siew Sin, who declared that there was no secession clause in the Malaysian constitution. Mr Lee retorted that secession clauses are seldom enshrined in constitutions but secessions still occurred when the people desired them. The Singapore Prime Minister realizes, however, that secession would be no solution for the island's, or his own, problems.

The imperative need of the hour would, therefore, require of Mr Lee to trim his sails for the stormy weather ahead. Malay suspicions about him being what they are, he will need both patience and tact to sail to his destination. In these qualities would lie Malaysia's salvation.

31

It is not all blood, sweat and tears in Indonesia's political and military confrontation of Malaysia. Confrontation has its lighter side which provides a welcome relief from the dreary and heartbreaking story of two lush green countries, inhabited for the better part by charming and friendly people, now in a state of undeclared war.

Indonesians are full of *joie de vivre* and although they are being subjected to a repetitious form of propaganda, their ebullience cannot be contained in political cliches. Apart from utilizing Radio Djakarta and, more particularly, the two secret anti-Malaysian radio stations for straight political propaganda, the Indonesian authorities spread sweetness and light through humour.

Indonesians have let it be known that 50 beautiful Malaysian girls had been operating as spies in the Rhio islands south of Singapore. High ranking officials were particularly asked to beware of this menace and the Djakarta authorities were immediately alive to the destructive capacities of Mata Haris. Political leaders warned that the Malaysian objective was to weaken Indonesia's resolve to pursue her confrontation policy.

While Djakarta's disclosure gave hopes to some in Malaysia that Indonesia would emulate the Malaysian example, the beautiful spies were soon forgotten in the excitement of Indonesian seaborne and air landings in Malaya. The episode, however, was too good to be thrown into oblivion and Djakarta, with its penchant for the dramatic, later doubled the number of beautiful Malaysian spies and distributed them among other parts of Indonesia.

There are great goings on over the two Indonesian-sponsored secret radio stations. Kalimantan Utara, a name which first gained currency during the Brunei revolt to denote the three Borneo States north of Indonesian Borneo, has its Prime Minister, Defence Minister and a whole set of representatives and plenipotentiaries exchanging messages and giving commands. Mr Azahari has now been resuscitated and signs impressive messages of congratulations, usually to President Soekarno.

Indonesia has also given Malaysia a new "Republic of Malaya" complete with an Acting President and Prime Minister. This "republic" has a liaison officer with jurisdiction over the Malayan peninsula and Singapore.

One of the two radio stations has broadcast a fascinating Indonesian analysis of the consequences of Mr Harold Wilson's election victory in Britain. Mr Lee Kuan Yew, it averred, was the "fair-haired boy" of Mr Wilson, a fellow Socialist, and consequently would replace Tengku Abdul Rahman as the country's leader. The Indonesians had found a comfortable house for the Tengku near London to which to send him to lead a retired life.

In spite of the fact that President Soekarno's last Independence Day oration was appropriately titled "Living Dangerously", the business of sending armed guerrillas and indoctrinated agents into Malaysia does not occupy all of Djakarta's time. Beatle and bird's nest hair styles and blue jeans come within the sweep of the Indonesian revolution. Police stations began with warnings that they would go to work with scissors on any mops they would discover on Indonesian heads. A group of girls sporting jeans and bird's nest hair styles was, in fact, taken to a police station and given a lecture on its deviation from the norms of crushing Malaysia.

A total of 106 girls wearing tight dresses and jeans were rounded up in Tjirebon, West Java, early in November. In Kediri, Central Java, police launched Operation Scissors to clip beatle hair styles to conformity; simultaneously, Indonesian women leaders were asked to form a Crush the Bird's Nest Hair Style movement. According to official reports, a team of police teachers and attorneys conducted something of a sociological investigation. Their finding was that girls with bird's nest hair styles were generally stupid in school and lazy at home; also, boys with beatle haircuts were going round the bend.

The twist has also been brought within the context of confrontation. Although Indonesians display much proficiency in dancing the twist, this dance is definitely discouraged. It is banned and those who disobey can be imprisoned. Police has been active rounding up "twisters": in Semarang, West Java, a group was let off after being warned. About 2,000 people demonstrated against the twist in Bandung. In Djakarta, police broke up a twist party early in November, arresting its organizer.

Efforts are now being made to replace the twist with the lenso, described as a slow rhythm blues and supposedly originated by President Soekarno. Dancers hold hands in the lenso and in a group form a circle round one person who chooses a partner, others then following suit.

The Crush Malaysia campaign is sought to be kept alive throughout these operations. In Djakarta, operations to combat mice were launched with shouts of "Crush the Imperialist Wrath! Crush Malaysia and Crush the Four-Legged Mice". Cabinet members' wives have been demonstrating their proficiency in giving first aid and organizing emergency kitchens as part of the Crush Malaysia programme and President Soekarno's ties have been auctioned to raise money for the same cause.

In one instance, however, Indonesians have shown a different genre of humour. They displayed a wry sense of humour in converting the former British Council building in Bandung into a library for the Dwikora, President Soekarno's twin command to "crush" Malaysia.

1965
THE BREAK—AND A COUP

32

In Malaysia, the air is thick with hopes of a rapprochement with Indonesia. Indonesian moves for peace in February and March and the activities of the growing community of mediators have struck a responsive chord in the hearts of the Malay leadership in Kuala Lumpur. But even among Malays there are differences on prospects of peace, while the Malaysian Chinese are plainly suspicious of Indonesian moves because they harbour the feeling that peace between Indonesia and Malaysia will be at the expense of their long-term interests.

The new Malaysian diplomatic approach to Indonesia is, however, as much a tactical move as it is motivated by a genuine desire for peace that exists, particularly among Malay leaders. The switch from the hard to the soft line became necessary to counter Indonesian peace offensives in many Asian capitals. Kuala Lumpur could not afford to sit idly by while Djakarta gave the world the impression that Malaysia was the stumbling block to peace.

Malaysia has won the latest round in peace diplomacy, with Djakarta asking for a postponement, on somewhat specious grounds, of the projected meeting in Bangkok between Tengku Abdul Rahman and President Soekarno. Peace continues to be the official watchword in Kuala Lumpur. A two-nation summit at Bangkok is not ruled out nor the idea of a meeting between the two leaders in Tokyo in May.

A meeting between President Soekarno and the Tengku can at best be the starting point of laborious negotiations at official and Ministerial levels unless a basis for a solution can be found beforehand. It has been the particular objective of Japanese diplomacy to make painstaking efforts to find a common denominator before irrevocably taking the hazardous road of mediation. This is a wise approach.

The four-nation Afro-Asian Conciliation Commission, accepted in principle by both Malaysia and Indonesia in Tokyo last summer, is an obvious starting point for negotiations. But the terms of reference of such a Commission will be a bone of contention between the two countries.

It is the Malaysian viewpoint that the sovereignty and independence of the Federation are not in doubt and the members of the Commission will, and must, be countries which have accepted the fact of Malaysia's existence. In Kuala Lumpur's view, therefore, the essential task of the Commission will be to conciliate, i.e., to help evolve a formula which will enable Indonesia to accept Malaysia as it stands.

This is an understandable approach since the Federation's negotiators cannot be expected to participate in talks which will lead to the liquidation of their troubled country. But it cuts across a primary aim of Indonesian confrontation, the break-up of Malaysia. The Indonesian objective, therefore, will be to arm the Commission with sufficient powers to recommend a process that could lead to the Federation's dissolution.

There is little meeting ground between these contradictory objectives unless Indonesia succeeds in finding acceptance for what could appear a face-saving formula, but which would ultimately work to Malaysia's disadvantage. However, if it is assumed that Indonesia will reconcile herself to Malaysia's existence for the immediate future, there would be scope for negotiations.

The primary aim of Indonesian foreign policy is to replace British power and influence in South-East Asia. The

British base in Singapore has, therefore, been a particular object of Djakarta's dislike. In the much-abused Manila Agreement of 1963, Indonesian negotiators succeeded in introducing the clause that all foreign bases in the area were temporary in nature. There is, however, no time limit set to the British base in Singapore and it is quite possible that Malaysia will be prepared to undertake to write in a time limit for the Singapore base (of between five and 15 years) in exchange for Indonesian recognition, with the proviso that Djakarta shows its respect for peace in the years to come.

A secondary point that has still to be cleared is whether the Philippines should be included in the projected talks between Indonesia and Malaysia. Kuala Lumpur wants bilateral talks because of its desire to isolate the Philippines' claim to Sabah from the issues posed by Indonesian confrontation. Besides, it feels that, in spite of President Macapagal's efforts to play a mediatory role, the equation in three-nation talks is inclined to be two to one against Malaysia. On the other hand, Indonesia might insist that the Philippines should sit in during the talks because they are the originators of the Conciliation Commission proposal apart from having been the host country for the 1963 Manila conference.

The mediators, principally Japan and Thailand, are building the edifice of the projected peace talks on the assumption that President Soekarno desires peace, unless a future meeting is to be a purely tactical Indonesian exercise in relation to the forthcoming Afro-Asian conference at Algiers. There are some indications why President Soekarno should be more desirous of peace now than before.

The struggle between the Indonesian Communist Party and non-Communists has sharpened. There are increasing signs of unrest in the Army at the growing power and influence of the PKI. The Communists' demand that peasants be armed to help Indonesian confrontation of Malaysia was probably made in the context of expected Chinese military aid to Indonesia. Dr Subandrio's visit to Peking was, in any event, far from an unalloyed success.

Official Indonesian reports also speak of moves in the Navy to replace Rear-Admiral Martadinata. The moves did not succeed, but are an indication of continuing Communist efforts to weed out persons in key positions whom they consider unreliable. The main naval base at Surabaya is located in a fertile stamping ground of the PKI.

While President Soekarno cannot create the impression of giving in completely to PKI pressures because he would thereby bring a showdown nearer, the military aspects of Indonesian confrontation have been far from successful. Politically, the confrontation has increased the stresses and strains in Malaysia but it would be futile to presume—Mr Lee Kuan Yew's pessimistic prognostications notwithstanding—that Malaysia is going to break up in the next few weeks. The long-term viability of Malaysia is, however, another matter.

There are about 50,000 British troops in the Malaysia theatre and Britain has no intention at present of withdrawing them for quite some time, unless a political solution makes their presence unnecessary. Besides, Australia and New Zealand are giving more than symbolic support to the Federation.

All these factors, coupled with the lack of sympathy shown by the better part of the world towards Indonesia's decision in January to leave the United Nations, would suggest that there are valid grounds for a change in Djakarta's policy. Presuming that some rethinking has been going on in Merdeka Palace, even a temporary rapprochement with Malaysia must have the acquiescence of the PKI. Japan is conscious of this factor, as evidenced by her Ambassador in Djakarta seeing the PKI Chairman, Mr D.N. Aidit. A reported version of this interview does not give grounds for hope.

There are few reasons why the PKI should agree to seek peace with Malaysia since its interests, as also China's, would seem to lie in continuing to create confusion and chaos in Indonesia and Malaysia. Malaysians believe that China recently linked her offer of arms aid to Indonesia to the latter continuing her confrontation policy. The battle for succession in a post-Soekarno Indonesia has already begun, and it seems that the PKI will remain content with softening up the country until it is confident it can take over.

Since the key to the settlement of the Indonesia-Malaysia dispute lies with Indonesia, the question thus boils down to President Soekarno's willingness and ability to outmanoeuvre the PKI by making it accept a limited period of peace. In seeking postponement of the projected Bangkok talks, the Indonesian Foreign Minister's letter implied that PKI pressures were the reason for the request. The odds would, indeed, seem against a rapprochement although President Soekarno's almost uncanny knack of doing the unpredictable lends a necessary element of hope to future talks that might be held between Indonesia and Malaysia.

33

In one of his more candid moments, the Malaysian Prime Minister mused in June that he wished he had not been persuaded by Mr Lee Kuan Yew about the island's eagerness to join Malaysia.

This tinge of regret about the transformation of Malaya from a happy and placid State into an object of confrontation from Indonesia on one hand and Mr Lee on the other is to be found among many members of the Tengku's United Malays National Organization in Kuala Lumpur. Regretfully, they acknowledge that Malaysia having been formed they have to put up with Indonesian confrontation and Mr Lee's relentless bid to capture power in Malaya.

The two problems are inter-related in the minds of UMNO leaders, as they are in reality. With Indonesia's continuing confrontation, UMNO is seriously limited in exercising its ultimate implied threat of the Malays being forced to find salvation by joining their kinsmen and co-religionists in Indonesia. You cannot successfully fight ideological and military belligerence of a neighbour and threaten to join the enemy's camp. Mr Lee Kuan Yew knows this and recently publicly pooh-poohed the idea in the following words: ". . . I am not going to take that threat, that they are going to give up all this black marble (allegedly in some Malays' bathrooms) to the Army commander that will come with the Siliwangi Division (of Indonesia)—not credible."

Indeed, the most striking change that has come about in the political atmosphere of Malaysia is that things that were till recently only whispered in private conversations now form the subject of public oratory. The debate between Mr Lee and his comrades in the People's Action Party on one hand and UMNO and its partners in Kuala Lumpur on the other often degenerates into mud-slinging and bitter personal attacks. But the issues being debated are weighty and the stuff of which Malaysia is made—the inter-racial complexion of its 11 million people.

Before entering into the debate, it would be useful to examine the basic characteristics of Malaya, the major component of the Malaysian Federation, and its constituent island State of Singapore. Politically, Malaya's development has been slow. The grant of independence in 1957 was a very civilized undertaking. Malaya retained the pyramid of the Paramount Ruler and the Sultans making them symbols and guardians of the State religion, Islam.

With Malays and Chinese divided in roughly equal numbers and Indians forming the third most important community, the economic predominance of the Chinese was offset by the Malays' political dominance. Malay rule prospered under the benign image of Tengku Abdul Rahman, immured by the comfortable foreign exchange earnings of tin and rubber which gave the country a standard of living far beyond the reach of most Asian nations. Politics was by and large a civilized affair played by gentlemen; the 12-year Emergency necessitated by Communist insurgency being quickly forgotten as a bad dream.

Singapore's political evolution has been very different. The island is a Chinese city and has been a hotbed of rebels, Communists and militant trade unionists. Mr Lee Kuan Yew's emergence to power in the State was remarkable for his ability to outmanoeuvre the Communists and bring the island into Malaysia under the guise of a referendum which was nothing of the kind.

Mr Lee now runs an efficient State Government, but although he calls himself a democratic socialist, the key distinction in a parliamentary democracy between the party in power and the State apparatus often does not exist for him. Singapore's radio and television are pressed into service for the greater glory of the People's Action Party at the time of elections and every day. Party speeches are distributed and publicized by the State Government apparatus and the island has a Minister of Culture, a euphemism for Minister of Propaganda. The State Assembly has met in recent times on an average once in six months.

It is clear that Malay leaders in Malaya did not fully realize the implications of Malaysia's formation. First, there were the heartaches of Indonesian confrontation, which cut across the devout wish of Malays for close relations with Indonesia; the moral prop provided by the existence of over 80 million Indonesian Malays to the Malays of Malaya immersed in a sea of Chinese became less tangible with confrontation. They bore the cross reluctantly.

However, for the Malay leaders a heavier cross to bear is Mr Lee Kuan Yew. PAP's decision to contest last year's general elections in Malaya raised a storm of protest; clearly, Malay leaders felt that Mr Lee had grossly violated the unwritten agreement on Malaysia's formation that he would remain within the island's political boundaries. They sadly underestimated Mr Lee's ambitions, but nevertheless set about to convince him that he should be content with making Singapore the "New York of Malaysia".

Mr Lee's decision to contest the elections ended in disaster; his party was soundly licked although it was working under the handicap of not opposing UMNO, concentrating its fire power on the latter's partner, the Malayan Chinese Association. The results proved to Mr Lee that his strategy was unworkable; besides, UMNO leaders had made it plain to him that his efforts to supplant the MCA in order to share power at the Centre would meet with their strong opposition.

Not to be deterred, Mr Lee has thrown a new challenge to UMNO and the MCA. A gathering of representatives of five political parties—the PAP, the United Democratic Party, the People's Progressive Party, the Sarawak United People's Party and the Machinda Party of Sarawak—met in Singapore to sign a charter on "Malaysian Malaysia". This is a statement of unexceptionable sentiments, expressing fears about the racial trends in Malay thinking and the parties' resolve to fight racial ideologies.

Significantly, this new alliance is itself largely a racial grouping. Essentially, the PAP is a Chinese party; so are the UDP with its base on Penang island, the PPP with its seat of power in the tin-mining Malayan State of Perak and the SUPP. The last was not so long ago described as being subversive (some of its sub-branches have been closed down under Central authority) and staunchly opposed Malaysia's formation. In reality, the grouping is tailored to suit Mr Lee's needs of acquiring the support of as many Chinese as he can to claim national leadership.

By running up the flag of "Malaysian Malaysia", Mr Lee hopes to emerge as a champion of a new Malaysian Chinese nationalism, since as an ethnic Chinese he realizes that he must first win Chinese support. His strategy, therefore, is immediately aimed at urban Chinese centres of power (in spite of the garb of multi-racialism he is careful to propagate), with an eye on the elections in 1969.

Mr Lee has at the same time deliberately stepped up the political debate. He has struck hard at Malay feelings and illusions. He has described the indigenousness of the Malays as a myth, picked holes in the Central Government's rural development plans, implied that if Malays did not give all citizens equal rights he would make "other alternative arrangements", implying, but never quite stating plainly, a partition of the country with the Chinese dominating Singapore, Penang, Malacca, Sabah and Sarawak. He has even taunted UMNO leaders with the remark that British troops would not continue to defend Malaysia if they wished to build a parochial nation.

Since Mr Lee declares almost every day that he "sits down with paper and pencil to calculate" each of his moves, the reactions to his pronouncements have been predictable. They have led to storms of protest and abuse from Malay leaders and newspapers, including demands for his arrest.

Mr Lee is now basking in the sun of these vituperations which have yielded him what he desired: additional proof of Malays' racialism and the rightness of his cause.

Mr Lee's slogan of "Malaysian Malaysia" has placed the more responsible of UMNO leaders on the defensive. They declare that this concept was in fact their creation, agreed to at the time of Malaysia's formation and even earlier. Special Malay political privileges such as reservation of jobs in Government service, land rights and special consideration in the grant of licences in commerce and industry are meant only to reduce the imbalance between Malay poverty and Chinese prosperity, they argue. (Mr Lee supports these privileges but describes them as irrelevant to the basic problem of bettering the Malays' lot.) UMNO leaders also taunt Mr Lee for his alleged opportunism, his alleged dictatorial methods in running his State Government, his alleged perfidy in fighting domestic battles abroad. On the last point UMNO leaders suspect that Mr Lee denigrates Central leaders on his trips abroad to gather international support for himself; since he talks in the modern idiom and is a dynamic leader, the outside world is inclined to equate these qualities with wisdom, much to the annoyance of Malays.

Malaysia is not an ideal secular democracy, particularly in the Malays' approach to many modern problems. But Mr Lee's new-found enthusiasm for shooting down Malay prejudices and weaknesses must lead to serious doubts about their repercussions, irrespective of the benefits they bring him. The racial cauldron being stirred so vigorously, by Mr Lee among others, can go on the boil, bringing down the house of Malaysia with it.

34

In the developing confrontation between Singapore and Kuala Lumpur, the resident foreign correspondent in Malaysia has become a subject of bitter dispute. Far from being allowed to do his work quietly, he constantly figures in Ministerial speeches and is a target of abuse or fulsome praise.

This is an unenviable position for the 20-odd full-time resident foreign correspondents. Unfortunately, they share the limelight with such political virtuosi as Mr Lee Kuan Yew or Dato Syed Ja'afar Albar of the United Malays National Organization. Indeed, there seems little hope that this larger-than-life image of the foreign correspondent will be set aside and that he will be permitted to do his work outside the spotlight of the local Press, radio and television.

Willy-nilly, the foreign correspondent in Malaysia has been dragged into the vortex of local politics in which it suits one side to build him up and the other to warn him and express resentment. The only course open to those of us who resist the temptation of becoming television stars of a somewhat lesser brilliance than Mr Lee is to wait and see—and, as a colleague put it to me, keep our bags packed.

This Malaysian obsession with the foreign correspondent received a fillip early in July with the expulsion of a Briton, Mr Alex Josey, who described himself as a freelance correspondent. To anyone familiar with the Singapore scene, Mr Josey occupied a position no other foreign correspondent could claim. His appearance was distinctive: he wore something approaching a Poincare beard and always donned a coloured batik bush-shirt for formal cocktail parties.

Mr Josey distinguished himself as Mr Lee Kuan Yew's part-time employee, and saw much of the world in the capacity of his Press relations officer. In Singapore, it was he who arranged who should interview Mr Lee at what time and he could open the locked doors of Ministerial silence.

The expulsion order served on Mr Josey on July 6 merely stated that his departure would be "conducive to the good of the Federation". He was given two weeks to depart. This was clearly a blow aimed at Mr Lee by the Central Government whose spokesmen, however, variously explained the action to the world. They said he had interfered in the internal affairs of the country, that he was "misusing Malaysia's hospitality" by promoting ill-will among the Chinese and Malay races, etc.

The expulsion provoked a torrent of criticism from a wide spectrum of the British Press from the *Times* to the *New Statesman*—a heartening phenomenon for those associated with newspaper work. But not one of the distinguished journalists who came to Mr Josey's rescue asked himself *the* question posed by the expulsion: can a foreign correspondent who was in the employ of one of the two parties to an internal dispute claim the privileges conferred upon him by his job? Perhaps, this was due to the incompetence with which Central Government spokesmen tried to cover up their unpopular action.

However, the uniformly critical tone of the British and Australian Press has had the unfortunate effect of further vitiating the atmosphere in which foreign correspondents have to work in Malaysia. Ironically, Mr Lee Kuan Yew and his People's Action Party, whose past record in relation to freedom of the Press in the country would make any responsible politician in the West blush, are now cast in the role of the Defender of the Foreign Correspondent. (Most of the 12 pages of an issue of the weekly PAP propaganda bulletin, *Malaysian Mirror*, published under the aegis of the Singapore Ministry of Culture, are devoted to Mr Josey who was feted by the Minister before his departure.) The Alliance Government, particularly its UMNO component, on the other hand, appears to the world in an unfavourable light.

The Alliance leaders' suspicion of the foreign correspondent takes us back at least a year ago when Malay-Chinese riots in Singapore broke the long truce between the two communities. Foreign Press comment on the riots placed most of the blame for the disturbances on certain elements in UMNO. These comments were promptly cyclostyled by Mr Lee's Minister of Culture and distributed through the State publicity apparatus.

The comments raised a clamour among sections of the Malay Press for the expulsion of Mr Josey and Mr Dennis Bloodworth of the London *Observer*—the latter had used a particularly piquant pen in blaming UMNO extremists. Criticism of Mr Bloodworth died its natural death, but *Utusan Melayu*, the Malay language newspaper closest to UMNO, periodically revived the demand for Mr Josey's expulsion. Among the alleged slights to his credit was his attempt to relate Malays' descent to a line of pirates.

Mr Lee Kuan Yew's own personality added fuel to this fire—as far as the Central leaders were concerned. Whatever his faults, he is a brilliant and perspicacious politician and because he is his own best public relations officer he has traditionally made a somewhat disproportionate impact on foreign correspondents, most of whom are based in Singapore. Many UMNO leaders thus acquired the view that foreign correspondents were for Mr Lee and, therefore, *per se* against them.

Against this background, it is easy to see why criticism of Central action in expelling Mr Josey merely went to reinforce Kuala Lumpur's suspicions. And in the present mood, many of them are only too prone to equate inaccurate or biased reporting, or simply unfavourable comment, with the foreign correspondent's imagined ulterior motives.

Yet, because of the circumstances involving Mr Josey's expulsion and the charm Mr Lee excercises on many foreign correspondents, no comment is now free from being misconstrued. In a speech to the Foreign Correspondents' Association in Singapore, the Malaysian Deputy Prime Minister, Tun Abdul Razak, made a commendable effort to set doubts at rest. He said the Central Government believed in freedom of the Press and would continue to permit "fair comment".

At the same time, Tun Razak appealed to the foreign Press to understand the peculiar difficulties of a young Federation which was facing Indonesian confrontation. Unfortunately, the phrase "fair comment" remained undefined—through no fault of his. No foreign correspondent rose to ask questions, in spite of Tun Razak's invitation.

Central Government spokesmen privately emphasize that foreign Press comment is reprinted in Malaysia and therefore excites feelings. They also explain that the level of sophistication reached by Western countries in taking unfavourable comment in their stride does not exist in the Federation. And they appeal to foreign correspondents to bear in mind these aspects when writing reports.

It is true that freedom of the Press in Malaysia does not have the connotations it has in Britain, the USA or India. Yet in South-East Asia, with the very honourable exception of the Philippines, no other country has the limited freedom of the Press Malaysia enjoys. It would be a tragedy if the present debate on the foreign correspondent should further limit Malaysia's horizons.

35

It is ironic that the man most responsible for bringing the turbulent island of Singapore into Malaysia should be most responsible for its unceremonial exit from the Federation. On August 9, after the surprise announcement of Singapore's separation from the rest of Malaysia, Mr Lee Kuan Yew broke down before television cameras.

Mr Lee is a very disappointed man today, and in his hour of anguish he deserves sympathy. The Singapore Prime Minister had brought to the Malaysian scene a dash of energy and drive rarely seen before. He has been a dynamo of power, both in taming Singapore and bringing it into the Malaysian fold through bluster and a highly suspect referendum, and in propagating his ideas about the kind of Malaysia that should come into being.

It is a tragedy that Mr Lee became so obsessed with his ideas and with projecting his personality before the whole of Malaysia and the world that he lost sight of the limitations of his environment. The writing on the wall was becoming clearer with each passing day: faced with a threat of their own extinction and that of their concept of Malaysia, the leaders of the Central Government were being increasingly driven to the wall. But Mr Lee chose to disregard the storm signals and forgot the first rule of a successful politician: never force your adversary into an impossible position, particularly one who has wide powers of action.

When the blow fell, Mr Lee was taken unawares; he was holidaying in a hill resort in Malaya. Tengku Abdul Rahman had returned home after a two-month sojourn abroad, necessitated by an attack of shingles, during the course of the previous week. And he let his Ministers broach the idea of Singapore's secession from Malaysia to some Singapore Ministers. Mr Lee was summoned by his colleagues to Kuala Lumpur to participate in perhaps the most fateful meetings of the People's Action Party.

From available accounts of these meetings, it seems that Mr Lee Kuan Yew had to fight hard to retain the leadership of his party because the only alternative to Singapore's eviction from Malaysia was to give the PAP a new leader. Mr Lee's instinct for political survival won the day—over the doubts of leaving the other members (spread over Malaya and Sarawak) of the Solidarity Convention, fathered by the PAP, rather in the lurch; over the strong feelings of many PAP Ministers about breaking up a logical and desirable partnership with Malaya.

The PAP was thus left holding the baby, i.e., Singapore. The success of the Central leaders' strategy lay in its element of surprise. The only reprieve possible was through the political exile of Mr Lee and once the PAP set its back on this idea, there was no alternative for it but to sign on the dotted line—to Singapore's separate independent existence.

Essentially, Mr Lee Kuan Yew failed in his objective because he gave Malay leaders in Malaya the impression that his ambitions knew no bounds and because he sadly miscalculated his adversaries' reactions. Logically, no sane Malaysian leader should have contemplated Singapore's secession when the new Federation's integrity had been made a vital centrepiece for resisting Indonesian subversion and infiltration. Such action can only hearten Indonesians and give rise to doubts in Sabah and Sarawak about their future in Malaysia.

The Tengku and other leaders of his United Malays National Organization chose to disregard these weighty reasons because they became increasingly convinced that Mr Lee would achieve a fair measure of success in Malaya, in the process sacrificing the interests of the Malays and their cherished goals. For them, the lesser of the two evils was Singapore's exclusion from Malaysia.

Singapore's separate existence raises two basic questions: one internal and the other external. As the almost jubilant reaction of a large number of the island's Chinese population indicates, Mr Lee's task in steering his party on a non-racial course will be a difficult one. Singapore is essentially a Chinese city and its first experience in managing its affairs independently will encourage pressures for a Singapore as a centre of Chinese nationalism in South-East Asia.

In foreign affairs, Mr Lee has already set his tiny country's course on a non-Communist Afro-Asian keel (he compared his concept of Singapore's survival with Prince Sihanouk's). He has also envisaged consular relations with Indonesia and the Eastern European countries and has indicated his country's desire to trade with everyone, South Africa excepted.

In following an independent foreign policy, however, Mr Lee has two serious limitations. One is the major British base on the island and the other the reactions of a differently orientated Malaysian Government to his policies. Both have a vital bearing on the island's survival.

The British base is not only militarily vital to a newly-born island nation which is intending to raise its first brigade but also to its economic survival. According to one estimate, about 25% of Singapore's income is derived from the existence of the base. This is so not in terms of the direct employment the base provides but because of the spending power of British troops and their families—in terms of housing, servants, food and other necessities and luxuries.

Second, Singapore's survival is closely connected with the rest of Malaysia, both in terms of trade and commerce and from the defence point of view. The island's trade with the rest of Malaysia forms nearly one-fourth of its total trade and Kuala Lumpur can make life very difficult for Singapore. The island's burgeoning industrial development was based on its easy access to the Malaysian market, and it would be extremely difficult for it to achieve quickly Hongkong's level of export of consumer goods to pay its way in the world.

Singapore will therefore have to trim its foreign policy to take into account the political liability of the British base on its soil and Malaysian susceptibilities. Neither of these problems is insurmountable, but they will require patient study and a subtle approach.

What can be the future of an island not even 32 square miles in area and a population of less than two million? Singapore's geographic location and its excellent port facilities are two points in its favour. The dreams of the Singapore business community for restoration of old trade ties with Indonesia are, however, likely to prove largely illusory. Having discovered the advantages of conducting trade on its own, Indonesia will be loath to give Singapore a substantial cut for its entrepot facilities, except for a political price.

There are thus built-in temptations for a ruling Singapore party to "trade with the devil" if need be for the country's survival, as Mr Lee put it at his first Press conference after the break with Malaysia. Mr Lee has also interlinked the question of Southern Malaya's defence with the necessity of having to obtain the island's water supply from there. He has wisely indicated that he will not play Malaysia against Indonesia.

These are admirable sentiments, but the question that should be on everyone's mind is: will Mr Lee Kuan Yew or his successor be strong enough to withstand internal and external pressures that will want to make the island a Chinese State in the heart of South-East Asia? Will Singapore, in fact, justify the fears of Malay politicians to become a "second Cuba"?

36

Kuala Lumpur is full of prognostications about Singapore's dramatic exit from Malaysia, as well it might. The different lines of reasoning add up to degrees of confusion, rather than knowledge, about what the future will bring.

The central fact posed by Singapore's separation is that it introduces an entirely new set of circumstances in Malaysia's relations with Indonesia and the rest of the world. Flowing from this are the changes in Britain's defence strategy in the Far East that must inevitably be hastened.

It must be plainly acknowledged that none of Malaysia's friends or allies can henceforth look upon mainland Malaya's present links with Borneo States as anything but expendable. Having presided over the partial break-up of the Federation, Tengku Abdul Rahman has thrown his trump card into Indonesia's lap.

It does not necessarily follow that the Borneo States will break away from Malaysia tomorrow. They have for the moment no attractive alternative to remaining within the truncated Federation; but once such an alternative is offered to them, it is more than likely that both they and Kuala Lumpur will agree to part company. One scheme being mooted by politicians from the oil-rich Sultanate of Brunei, which stayed out of Malaysia at the last minute, is an independent Federation of Brunei and the Malaysian Borneo States.

This proposal has some obvious snags but it is not impossible of achievement. There will be opposition to the tiny State's overlordship of Sabah and Sarawak; the Sultan of Brunei himself is far from averse to reviving his ancestors' sway over the other two Borneo States. If such a federation comes into being, it could only survive under Indonesia's umbrella because any significant British military presence there will lead to another Indonesian confrontation.

Ironically, Mr Azahari's old dream of "Kalimantan Utara" could come to fruition in spite of the miserable failure of his Indonesian-backed revolt in December, 1962.

Indonesians would then be able to prove to the world that their combination of ideological propaganda, subversion, infiltration, economic boycott of Malaysia and bluster is a highly successful mixture.

There is, of course, the Philippines' claim to Sabah, an issue now susceptible to some intriguing twists. One way of throwing a spanner in the works—as far as future peace in South-East Asia is concerned—would be to give in to the claim. This would lead to a direct confrontation between Indonesia and the Philippines and would bring into play the American military presence in the latter country. Since the Philippines itself can hardly desire such a development, its claim could become an increasing source of embarrassment to President Macapagal.

However, from his own point of view, Tengku Abdul Rahman might yet prove to be entirely right in taking the snap decision to break with Singapore if it hastens a rapprochement between Malaya and Indonesia. It was becoming clearer every day that Malay leaders in Kuala Lumpur had not bargained for the tribulations Malaysia brought in its wake. They looked forebodingly at local Chinese efforts to capture power in the country. And since Malaysia's continuing existence only promised an indefinite British military presence and a permanent state of enmity with their kinsmen in Indonesia, it was perhaps understandable that the Tengku and his close associates looked upon the partial break-up of Malaysia as the lesser of the two evils.

To the Malays, at any rate, the present Malaysian Federation can hardly make sense because the essential purpose of including the Borneo territories was to balance the unwelcome Chinese majority Singapore's entry into the Federation would have brought about. With this essential purpose now non-existent, Malays will not be particularly enthusiastic about continuing to provide money indefinitely for the sorely-needed economic development of Borneo while continuing to invite Indonesian confrontation.

An undercurrent of resentment against Britain is indeed evident among Malays. Since London inspired and helped to form Malaysia including Singapore, it is understandable that Malays should want to transfer their frustrations, caused by Indonesian confrontation and Mr Lee Kuan Yew's policies, to the British. Open British admiration for Mr Lee buttressed Malay suspicions, which had been receiving much encouragement from Indonesian propaganda.

It is likely that with Singapore's exit from Malaysia, anti-British sentiment among Malays will grow. The break has certainly opened the door to a reconciliation between Malays and Indonesians although it has in the process created the problems posed by an independent Chinese State in the heart of South-East Asia. No amount of rationalization by Mr Lee Kuan Yew can disguise the fact that Singapore is essentially a Chinese State with a population having a propensity towards the People's Republic of China.

Britain's essential interest in Malaysia and Singapore is twofold. Malaya's rubber and tin resources will continue to provide an incentive for London's efforts to help maintain it as a Western-oriented country. Second, Singapore's strategic and excellent harbour facilities are essential to Britain's needs to keep the trade route to the Far East open.

While Britain is therefore likely to continue to maintain its bases in Singapore for as long as practicable, its decision will depend upon the economic penury its loss would bring to the island rather than on purely military considerations. Singapore has yet to prove that it can survive as a viable independent State and it will be in Britain's interest to give it whatever economic assistance it can to keep the island's head above water.

Neither of these two main British objectives should require the retention of the Borneo States within a truncated

Malaysia. But Britain will obviously have to balance the possible loss of the Borneo States and Brunei to an independent Federation under Indonesia's sphere of influence against the costs of a practicable alternative scheme. It goes without saying that, faced with financial difficulties, Mr Harold Wilson will use Singapore's break as a starting point in rationalizing his country's defence commitments in the Far East.

While the long-term implications of the dramatic developments in Malaysia are thus beginning to emerge, the short-term goals of the Powers involved are not yet clear. Both Indonesia and Britain seem to be waiting for the other side to make the first move before determining their own immediate strategy. President Soekarno did not oblige Britain in his Independence Day address on August 17 and it is likely that London will have to make a first tentative move to determine its future pattern of power and influence in South-East Asia.

For the present, however, Britain, Malaysia and Singapore are immersed in a sea of technicalities in giving effect to the island's separate existence. Between Malaysia and Singapore these technical problems are overlaid with a thick coating of mutual suspicions and acrimony.

37

The world can ignore recent happenings in Malaysia at its peril. While the immediate outlook following Singapore's separation from Malaysia can bring many nations little comfort, this event should provide an ideal starting point for framing the guidelines of future policy.

Singapore's break highlights the fact that Indonesian-Malay nationalism is the strongest indigenous force in South-East Asia. This is particularly so because the impasse in Vietnam means that a unified Communist Vietnam providing its own impetus cannot come into being until after the end of the carnage, peace and the long process of rebuilding on the ravages of war.

It is unfortunate that recent developments in Indonesian policy have taken an unsavoury turn. Only future historians can unravel precisely why President Soekarno chose to pursue a policy of confrontation when, with patience, he could have achieved his goals otherwise. Perhaps the orientation of his mind forced him to look for dramatic solutions rather than a more gradual policy.

However, in spite of all the unprincipled moves Indonesia has made and her tactical alignment with China, she remains the inspiration for dynamic nationalism in the region. This nationalism is built around the Malay race—stretching from Southern Thailand to the Philippines—and contains strands of Islam and a strong, if mixed-up, radicalism. The mixture, as events will prove in the future as they have in the past, is a heady brew for some 150 million people in South-East Asia.

The only other prevailing dynamic force in the area is provided by Chinese Communism, built around the rather small (some 12 million) but effective overseas Chinese population. The fact that Peking has so assiduously worked to woo Indonesia is clear proof of the present weakness of this force.

Chinese communities in South-East Asia are looked upon with suspicion by the indigenous people as any prosperous and closely knit immigrant community in a sea of local want is bound to be. Moreover, Chinese Communism, particularly when aligned with an alien minority, is an alien creed—in this garb unacceptable to the bulk of the people.

The motivations of China's leaders in closely working with Indonesia therefore become clear. They are riding on the crest of Indonesian nationalism because alone they cannot gain acceptance. Chinese leaders are only following the old adage that when you cannot beat the enemy, join him.

Both Peking and Djakarta, however, recognize that theirs is essentially a marriage of convenience; neither side expects it to last. Indonesia needs China for her own reasons. Having broken most of the rules of international conduct, Djakarta must perforce go to the most radical of the rule-breakers in the world for moral and some material support.

Once Indonesia achieves her aim of "crushing" Malaysia, Indonesia will seek to plough her path in international affairs alone. She can then once again afford to become a respectable member of the international community. This would be true even if Indonesia were to go Communist, because for Communism to succeed there, it would have to be Indonesian, principally Javanese, Communism having its own centre of interest away from Peking.

It is in this context that a Chinese Singapore's creation as an independent identity is of such tremendous import for China. For the first time Peking is promised a firm base in South-East Asia around which to spread its messianic message. As Mr Lee Kuan Yew's tears and his people's joy over the break-up of Malaysia amply demonstrated, it is a question of time before Singapore will become an unadorned Chinese State.

Although Mr Lee may yet continue to play an important role, there is no place for him as a nationalist leader in the future. The rising wave of Indonesian-Malay nationalism and an extreme form of Chinese nationalism will inundate him.

Against this background, it is imperative to begin a re-examination of relations between the nations of South-

East Asia and the world. What is being suggested is not opportunistic reversals of policy, a narrow and barren road, but a look beyond the dark present into the future.

38

The Indonesian crisis has at once demonstrated the strength and weakness of President Soekarno's dramatic stewardship of his country. The strength lies in the fact that, in spite of the coup of October 1 and the counter-coup and the stresses and strains they have produced, no significant regional revolt has broken out in the outer islands.

This is a remarkable achievement because the sprawling Indonesian islands, with their own dialects and prejudices against both Central and Javanese rule, have for long been prey to dissident tendencies. Dr Soekarno has thus given striking proof of having been able to impose an Indonesian identity on his far-flung country, whatever the future might hold.

The weakness of President Soekarno's rule has been all too evident from the present crisis, whose results have initially followed copybook predictions. Briefly, Dr Soekarno's method of maintaining his unique rule was to balance the Communist and non-Communist forces while imposing a hazy Marxism diluted with large doses of chauvinism.

Circumstances and Dr Soekarno's natural bent for slogans had been producing a peculiar environment in Indonesia in recent years. The result of these factors was that the very balance the President had been maintaining was tilting towards the Communist component of NASAKOM, with the nationalist and religious forces counting for less and less. It was therefore inevitable that when the opportunity occurred, as it did on October 1, the Armed Forces, particularly the Army, and the religious parties (in effect the Muslims) should set about righting the balance in their favour. The "nationalist" forces represented by the PNI were either mute or moribund.

It was widely assumed, and with good reason, that once President Soekarno disappeared from the Indonesian scene, the edifice of NASAKOM—embodying the concept of the unity of Communist, nationalist and religious forces—would come crashing down. With President Soekarno's failing health, jockeying for position had already begun during the past year. Dr Subandrio, the clever First Deputy Prime Minister and Foreign Minister, had been making himself acceptable to the Indonesian Communist Party in the hope that he would be the next President after Dr Soekarno.

Dr Subandrio's were shrewd tactics because the PKI was not strong enough to assume control over the country, as its recent misdemeanours have only too plainly proved, and it was reasonable to assume that the Communists would welcome a pliable "front man" to assume the Presidency while they would soften the ground further before taking over.

What were the circumstances that negated President Soekarno's shrewd but short-term policy of balancing the different forces? Plainly, the President's own concept of NASAKOM was becoming more and more lopsided. The PKI was increasingly in the position of being able to dictate to him on many key issues. The life of the Body for the Promotion of Soekarnoism, an effort by the non-Communist forces to correct the balance, was significantly brief. The Murba Party, a Trotskyist group with which the Third Deputy Prime Minister, Mr Chairul Saleh, was associated, was banned. And the witch hunt for non-Communists in key organizations was being carried out effectively. The Communists had also set about preparing in earnest the arming of peasants while infiltrating the Armed Forces.

First, there are limitations in President Soekarno's own make-up. His contribution to the building of modern Indonesia is unique and striking. His major achievement has been the holding together of the sprawling Indonesian islands. Dr Soekarno has proved a charismatic leader loved by his people and capable of inducing great bursts of energy in them.

When that is said, President Soekarno has proved singularly inept in promoting any significant measure of economic reform or far-sightedness in building for the future. As some of Dr Soekarno's Cabinet Ministers have told me in Djakarta in the past, they would have to wait for another President before economic objectives are not constantly sacrificed to grandiose political considerations. Dr Soekarno plainly has no head or patience for economics and its relevance to the country's future.

Another factor in President Soekarno's make-up is his radicalism and vague Marxism. He is a true nationalist but his nationalism has become overlaid with a fuzzy aura of cliches which are good as far as they go, but become particularly harmful when substituted as measures of policy.

With the Indonesian genius for presenting difficulties as assets, it has always been proudly claimed that since over 70% of Indonesia's economy was in the non-monetized sector, inflation and the ridiculous depths to which the Indonesian rupiah had sunk were of little concern. As evidence of people's difficulties and dissatisfaction mounted in the cities in the recent past, even ebullient Indonesians had to change their tune to acknowledge some of the difficulties—without making a concerted effort to obviate them.

Apart from the limitations imposed by President Soekarno's flamboyant and political personality, the formation of Malaysia has played a crucial part in turning him towards PKI and Peking in seeking salvation for his country. Although it is conceivable that China would have benefited from the circumstances of Indonesia's political evolution, its dramatic advances symbolically date from Indonesia's rejection of the UN report on the Borneo territories.

The event of Malaysia's formation and the Indonesian decision to confront the new Federation set President Soekarno on a path that could only lead his country to the embrace of Peking. It is still not clear why the President rejected the UN report after promising to abide by it at the Manila conference of 1963; Dr Subandrio had a role to play in this decision. Once it was taken, the winds from the now burnt-out office of the PKI, encouraged by Peking, could blow the country in only one direction.

Before the October 1 coup attempt, the PKI had almost succeeded in forcing Indonesia to break off relations with the USA after cleverly guiding anti-British feeling into anti-American expressions, in line with China's policy of regarding America as "Enemy Number One". The withdrawal from the UN was so enthusiastically welcomed by Peking that even Dr Subandrio felt constrained to stress his country's belief in the principles of the Charter. American economic aid had become a casualty long ago in the forest of Indonesia's resolve to crush Malaysia.

Clearly, President Soekarno's three-legged race to revolution—in the form of NASAKOM—was becoming increasingly a partnership between him and the PKI. Even if this were not so, the concept of NASAKOM was bound to founder after his demise because it was held together by a cement of cliches kept in place by himself. Radicalism is not a virtue in itself unless it is coupled with purposeful policies of social welfare, even in as potentially rich and temperate a country as Indonesia.

Even for President Soekarno, who has officially adopted the slogan of "living dangerously", recent events must have proved unpalatable. Although it seems likely that he will succeed in resuscitating a pale version of NASAKOM out of the ashes of the coup and counter-coup, he will have postponed a catastrophe, not averted it.

In the twilight years of his life therefore President Soekarno will be saddened in the knowledge that his amalgam of Marxism and Javanese nationalism has not survived his own lifetime. The Army has gained much from the abortive coup; the PKI has lost perhaps as many as five to 10 years in its march towards power. A civil war has for the present been averted but living dangerously as a cult has failed to answer the needs of Indonesia.

39

Independent Singapore's first 100 days are an indication of the kind of problems the new State will face—and pose to the world. As Mr Lee Kuan Yew has confessed, there were first the rather trivial but trying problems of setting up shop.

Very few Singapore citizens possessed a knowledge of French, and help had to be sought from some very unconventional sources to deal with Cambodia and the French-speaking African States. Then people had to be drilled in the secrets of coding and decoding State messages. And Mr S. Rajaratnam, a Ceylonese by descent, found himself with a brand new Foreign Ministry consisting of one person —himself.

It must be said to the credit of the Singapore Government that it remains undeterred by these sudden problems—

sudden because Singapore's eviction from Malaysia was a snap decision. After sending messages to as many heads of States as he had previously shaken hands with, Mr Lee Kuan Yew impatiently waited for formal recognition.

Recognition was, in many cases, slow in arriving, leading to much distress in City Hall, the home of Government offices in Singapore. Mr Lee suffered a breakdown in the process and was persuaded by his colleagues to take a short holiday. Meanwhile, messages of formal recognition slowly trickled in, although Indonesia, China and Pakistan (probably in concert) did not recognize Singapore.

The 31.5-square-mile island State of Singapore is now duly installed in the United Nations with Russian tolerance, and is in the Commonwealth in spite of Pakistan's abstention. It has been accorded recognition by the major radicals in Africa, including Guinea and Ghana.

One of the first steps taken by the independent Singapore Government was to send out a Ministerial mission to a number of countries in Africa and Asia. The object of this exercise was to convince the world that, in spite of the major British base on its soil, Singapore was not neocolonial (a word made famous by Indonesian propaganda) or a British stooge. Mr Lee seems to be obsessed by the fact that he will be misunderstood and misrepresented on this point and many of his major pronouncements since independence have sought to dispel the world's doubts.

The two major problems facing independent Singapore have been correctly defined by Mr Lee Kuan Yew—a voluble, vocal and sometimes indiscreet Prime Minister. They are the physical survival of the island, and trade, on which the economic prosperity of Singapore depends. The two problems are closely inter-related because Mr Lee's own future and the State's policies will depend upon the measure of prosperity he can give his newly-independent country.

At home Mr Lee and his People's Action Party have set about proclaiming a multi-racial policy. Although the Chinese comprise nearly 80% of the island's population of 1.8 million, Malay has been retained as the national language. Chinese, together with Tamil and English, are to be the three other official languages. Mr Lee has also promised constitutional safeguards for the minorities; the constitution is to be rewritten for the purpose, although it remains to be seen whether he will, in the process, succumb to the temptation of becoming an executive President.

There are very valid reasons for Mr Lee's attachment to multi-racialism, in spite of the fact that it is patently absurd for an independent country to adopt the language of a minority. Mr Lee did not knowingly invite Singapore's dramatic eviction from Malaysia although his actions led to it. And he is so committed to the "Malaysian Malaysia" slogan he propagated before the separation that he has little option but to carry it forward.

It is difficult to say whether Mr Lee really believes in Singapore's reunion with Malaysia, even in 15 years' time. To the outsider, this slogan is beginning to sound like the proclaimed conviction of the Nationalist Chinese to reconquer the mainland. However, it is obviously in Mr Lee's interest to keep alive the myth because otherwise his whole edifice of multi-racialism will collapse, probably bringing him down with it.

In international affairs, Mr Lee's preoccupation has been with selling Singapore as a non-aligned country, the British base notwithstanding. He has succeeded in doing so to a remarkable extent, although many African leaders in particular will judge Singapore's performance by its future actions—particularly the duration of the base. In other respects, Mr Lee will not be found wanting in expounding popular, if now somewhat dated, theories of Afro-Asianism.

Singapore's relations with Malaysia are crucial to the island's happiness and it is in this field that Mr Lee has met his most serious reverse. Admittedly, Mr Lee's reputation in Kuala Lumpur being what it is, it would have been an uphill task to heal the wounds of the past year's controversies. Besides, Kuala Lumpur has been in no frame of mind to soften the blow of separation, particularly because Mr Lee continues to run Singapore.

On the other hand, Mr Lee has not found it possible to repress his contempt for many of the social and other values prevailing in Kuala Lumpur. This has occasioned two strong protest notes from Malaysia, rightly charging him with interference in a foreign country's internal affairs. The Singapore Government is now adopting the argument that the island's defence commitments for Malaysia are parallel with the Federation's promise of co-operation in economic affairs.

Although Singapore is trying to use its desire to resume barter trade with Indonesia as a bargaining lever to extract trade concessions from Malaysia, Mr Lee's intemperate speeches are hardly likely to mellow tempers in Kuala Lumpur. Continuing dissension between the island and the Federation can therefore be expected.

Indeed, Mr Lee has given particular evidence in recent months of an emotional streak in his character. Nowhere is this revealed more clearly than in his public pronouncements about the USA. It is, of course, permissible for Mr Lee to take a swipe at the favourite whipping boy of Afro-Asia to prove his non-alignment, but his methods and his persistence can scarcely rebound to his credit.

Less than three weeks after Singapore's separation from Malaysia, Mr Lee chose a long monologue during a television Press conference to bring up the dramatic charge of a US Central Intelligence Agency agent caught in the act of bribing a Singapore police officer in 1960. He disclosed that he promised to keep quiet about the affair if the USA paid M$ 100 million to the Singapore Government for the island's economic development, but was offered only M$ 10 million for himself and his People's Action Party. The offer was angrily rejected although the affair was subsequently hushed up.

Mr Lee's purpose in bringing up this matter some five years after it happened was perhaps to balance the fact of his dependence on the British base with striking up an anti-American posture, particularly with an eye on pleasing China. The US State Department's denial of Mr Lee's charge was foolish; Mr Lee retorted by circulating photostat copies of Mr Dean Rusk's letter of apology, dated April 15, 1961. Although Mr Lee won the point, he might have done damage to his infant country's future in the process.

Another reason for Mr Lee's new habit of denigrating the Americans is his fear that as British disillusionment with their defence role East of Suez grows, the USA will partly fill the vacuum. The visits of the South Korean and South Vietnamese Prime Ministers to Kuala Lumpur have distressed him, as also the existence of a lobby in the Malaysian Chinese Association in Kuala Lumpur pressing for closer ties with Taiwan.

Lately, Mr Lee has been making it clear that his anti-Americanism is not entirely a measure of expediency but is a deeply-rooted prejudice. Among the compliments he has paid Americans are: The Americans are not wise; they lack depth and finesse. "Even (President) Kennedy didn't have the (quality of) full maturity". ". . . One thing they (Americans) cannot buy; and that is a corps of men who understand human beings and human situations". ". . . I have told them (Americans) this officially, to their officials—I said 'Look, you know nothing about this place' ".

The Indonesian attitude of wait and see in regard to Singapore has disappointed the island's leaders. With economic co-operation between Singapore and Malaysia bogged down in continuing recriminations, Mr Lee particularly wanted to open up Indonesian trade. In spite of making overtures to Djakarta by declaring that the British base was meant only for defence purposes and would not be permitted to be used for aggression on neighbours, the Singapore leaders got little change. And his proposal to resume barter trade with Indonesia on a limited scale was as much a sop to the business community in Singapore as it was a challenge to Kuala Lumpur.

Singapore's relations with China have followed an interesting pattern. Although Peking has not recognized Singapore, probably in deference to Indonesian wishes, China has given indirect praise to Singapore by blaming Kuala Lumpur for the separation and expressing pleasure that the Bank of China in Singapore would continue to operate. The Federal Government had ordered its closure before Singapore's break—a decision reversed by Mr Lee. China has also taken particular care not to rock the Singapore boat by word or action, lately even re-entering the Singapore rubber market after a year's absence.

By including Yugoslavia and the Soviet Union in their travels, members of Singapore's goodwill mission were following a sensible policy of opening a communications link with East Europe. (Neither Malaysia nor Singapore has diplomatic relations with any Communist country although both have recently expressed a vague desire to do so.) One result of the mission's visit to Moscow was agreement in principle on establishing a Russian rubber-buying mission and a Tass news agency office in Singapore.

Mr Lee has recently taken particular care to profess friendship for India. He was obviously pleased with New Delhi's quick action in formally recognizing the island—the first non-European Commonwealth country, apart from

Malaysia, to do so. But India serves a deeper purpose in his present difficulties; apart from winning the sympathy of Indians in Singapore (a little over 7% of the population), he can buttress his theories of multi-linguism and multi-religion by drawing on Indian experience.

The opportunistic nature of Mr Lee's new-found interest in India need not be a deterrent to New Delhi reciprocating Singapore's present warmth. But it would be dangerous to become sentimental about these bonds, particularly because Mr Lee will have to keep quiet, if not support China, on any Sino-Indian controversy. And one has only to live in Singapore for a time to know of the anti-Indian prejudice that prevails on the island in many sectors—notwithstanding official protestations to the contrary. In reacting to Singapore's new friendliness, New Delhi has also to take account of the extent to which it can afford to damage its relations with Malaysia; the drawing together of India and Singapore will have inevitable repercussions in Kuala Lumpur.

All in all, Mr Lee Kuan Yew can point to some successes to offset the failures he has had to encounter during his first 100 days of office in an independent Singapore. His gravest problems will remain at home; as the recent agitation for making Chinese the official language indicates, his brand of multi-racialism will be under constant attack. His success will depend upon his ability to keep the dollars flowing.

Mr Lee's trump card is that there is no non-Communist alternative to him in Singapore. It will, therefore, be in Britain's interest to keep the base going for a number of years, and for Australia and other Western countries, including the USA, to keep the island's head above water through trade and aid. Anyone acquainted with Mr Lee will know that he will extract the last dollar from the circumstances of Singapore's usefulness to the West. But his propensity to overplay his hand, combined with his desire to cut a dashing figure on the world stage, will continue to create crises. Tengku Abdul Rahman has already termed him a second Castro. A second Cuba is, in any event, preferable to having a third China—but it remains to be seen whether Mr Lee can stay in power long enough to stave off Chinese pressure, both at home and from Peking.

40

Neither Singapore's eviction from Malaysia nor the coup in Indonesia changes the long-term outlook for South-East Asia. Rather, they underline the projections of the past. But the timing of these momentous developments was a surprise, and the immediate outlook is a new factor to be reckoned with.

The Peking-Djakarta axis has cracked sooner than one would have expected. The basic differences between Singapore and Kuala Lumpur have led to an immediate divorce, not a separation. In the background, the Vietnam conflict has moved away from the possibility of an American military defeat, although victory is not within Washington's grasp.

It can be safely assumed that the American commitment to South Vietnam will continue in some form for the next five years, whether there are peace negotiations or not. The other two main crises in South-East Asia will, therefore, be unfolded in relative insulation from formidable direct Chinese pressures. Thailand is one country where the Chinese can do some effective sniping, but Thailand's is a relatively long-term problem.

The fate of a large part of South-East Asia will thus largely be decided by indigenous factors although outside pressures, particularly from the Great Powers, will have their impact. The crises in Singapore, Malaysia and Indonesia are, in fact, various facets of a central problem: how will the antagonisms between the Malay and Chinese races be resolved against the background of Indonesia's ambitions as the major indigenous power?

The Communists' present ignominy in Indonesia and the acquisition of strength by the Army and Muslim organizations have brought the prospect of a political understanding between the Republic and the Malays of Malaya nearer. Singapore's multi-racial policy is fashioned to ensure Mr Lee Kuan Yew's political survival as also to project an extremely unlikely reunion with the Federation.

Behind Singapore's dubious experiment in multi-racialism, however, lies a much larger and more portentious question: can multi-racialism survive in Malaysia? The winds of change Mr Lee Kuan Yew introduced into Malaysia with such impetuosity, leading to Singapore's unceremonious exit from the Federation, are still blowing in and around Kuala Lumpur. Malaysia's opposition spokesmen have adopted Mr Lee's philosophy and tactics to buffetthe Alliance Government in debate while Singapore now stands on the sidelines, subtly and otherwise cheering them on.

Will these onslaughts on the Malays' style of doing things in Malaysia snap their patience to hasten the process of a political union with Indonesia? A first step towards this could be a deal on the Borneo States, the main bone of contention between the two. Indonesia has, significantly, started talking again about Maphilindo.

In such circumstances, the Chinese in Singapore and Malaysia, feeling threatened by the onslaught of Malay chauvinism as the Malays now feel threatened by the Chinese, could call upon Peking for support. Singapore's independence will ensure that the Chinese will have a secure base of operation; Britain will have neither the will nor the resources to buttress the Chinese in Singapore against a joint Malay-Indonesian opposition. Even otherwise, the indigenous forces represented by Indonesians and Malays would be fighting an alien force and would, therefore, have an advantage in the struggle.

This glimpse into a hypothetical future proves a basic factor in South-East Asia's present turbulence; the winds of Malay-Indonesian nationalism are likely to prevail over others. Given Indonesia's radicalism, minus its Peking oriented Communism, one can only hope that the religious element in this future coming together of Malays and Indonesians will not dominate their political thinking. The Philippines' association with them in a resuscitated Maphilindo would be particularly useful because of the Philippines being a predominantly Roman Catholic country.

1966
PEACE?

41

Is Maphilindo dead and buried? Even when the concept was brought into being in the murky atmosphere of the Manila summit conference of the three countries in the summer of 1963, few expected it to take wing in the foreseeable future.

There were too many contradictions between the three countries in their political attitudes, content and style of Government, ideals and expectations. But it was then assumed, with good reason, that the concept of bringing together the Malay races in the three countries would fire the imagination of the leaders and would remain a beacon, however distant.

Although ex-President Macapagal of the Philippines gave some practical shape to Maphilindo, the concept was not new. Indonesians had thought of it in egocentric terms of a Greater Indonesia. Malay leaders, principally of the opposition Pan-Malayan Islamic Party, had dreamed of the coming together of the Malay races stretching from Southern Thailand to the Philippines. And Mr Macapagal, anxious to project his country into the neighbouring world of Asia, espoused it with great perseverance and fortitude.

Malaya's (later Malaysia's) public commitment to Maphilindo, it is true, was more muted than its partners'. Tengku Abdul Rahman had taken the precaution of including a leader of the Malayan Chinese Association in his team to the Manila summit conference. The objective was to commit the Chinese in Malaya (almost as numerous as the Malays) to the concept, which had obvious racial overtones.

Privately, however, Malay leaders and officials were as enthusiastic about Maphilindo as their counterparts in the other two countries. The reactions of the Malaysian Chinese were quite different. They harboured barely concealed suspicions about the concept.

Indonesia's confrontation of Malaysia was itself a dramatic negation of Maphilindo, although Indonesian officials described their action as a mere tactical deviation. The travails of confrontation gave the Chinese in Malaysia the chance to speak up against Maphilindo. Singapore's Prime Minister did so in no uncertain terms, condemning it as a racial concept.

Chinese opposition to Maphilindo was understandable since it was, not without reason, interpreted by them as a mechanism to hem them in. More surprising, however, is Tengku Abdul Rahman's body blow at Maphilindo in January. Next only to Indonesia's confrontation, the Tengku's attack has harmed a scheme which could have provided a counterweight to Chinese power and influence in South-East Asia.

The Tengku, it is true, did not condemn the concept's basic ideals. Rather, he related its birth to Malaysia's misfortunes, particularly in the form of Indonesian confrontation. Secondly, he said the concept would encourage the domination of the smaller countries (Malaysia and the Philippines) by the bigger one (Indonesia).

The Tengku has chosen to go against the grain of Malay feelings by rejecting Maphilindo. At the same time he has given much evidence of a new enthusiasm for the Association of South-East Asia, the economic and cultural grouping comprising Thailand, the Philippines and Malaysia. ASA faded into virtual non-existence in 1963 when the Philippines and Malaysia ceased to have diplomatic relations because of the former's legal claim to Malaysian Sabah. The new Philippine President, Mr Ferdinand Marcos, has now promised to normalize relations.

It is significant that the Tengku's rejection of Maphilindo comes at a time when events in Indonesia hold prospects of a rapprochement between the two countries. Why should the Tengku then choose to turn away from Indonesia?

It seems that the Tengku and the ruling Malay elite in Malaya have come to the conclusion that any close association between their country and Indonesia will work against the interests of their class. Whatever the regime in power in Djakarta, the radical mores of life and politics are likely to continue in Indonesia; these factors will no doubt exert pressures on Malaya in proportion to the closeness of links between Djakarta and Kuala Lumpur.

To be sure, the Malay leaders' decision to turn their backs on Maphilindo is a short-term solution. By doing so, they have acquired a greater interest in maintaining the peculiar structure of Malay political dominance with the symbolism provided by the Sultans in a very mixed and otherwise Chinese-dominated environment. The Chinese and others in the country (the two Borneo States of Sabah and Sarawak are a special and peripheral problem in this context) will continue to enjoy the benefits of prosperity as long as they accept the present Malay mores—and do not demand a greater say in framing policy.

This attempt to have the cake and eat it is bound to prove unworkable in the long run. By virtue of their decision, the Malay rulers cannot effectively use their threat of a union with Indonesia to ward off insistent Chinese demands for a place in the sun. At the same time, the leaders of the United Malays National Organization will be giving a valuable weapon to the opposition Right-wing PMIP to woo the Malay voters.

The Association of South-East Asia is no substitute for Maphilindo because, as it stands, it is a restricted economic rather than a political grouping among like-minded anti-

Communist ruling hierarchies of three countries. It seems hardly likely that Indonesia will join ASA to lend it political substance. (Thailand, it must be noted, has never been happy about Maphilindo because of the pressures the concept could exert on its southern Muslim provinces.)

ASA is essentially a gentlemen's club. It is a non-starter in the broader context of a viable grouping of South-East Asian nations which can hold its own against Chinese influence and power. Anti-Communism as such is, in any event, likely to prove a sterile road. The Tengku, having thrown the baby with the bathwater, is merely reiterating his interest in the *status quo* in a region where the winds of change are blowing fiercely.

The major Western Powers in the area, Britain and the USA, seem reconciled to, if not content with, the collapse of Maphilindo. (The USA particularly was at one time a fervent advocate of the ideal.) It is, therefore, now left to the Soviet Union to help encourage a regional grouping which can provide the necessary nationalistic urge to maintain its larger independence. Recent events in Indonesia, particularly the diminishing of Chinese influence, are a good augury. Indonesia is, indeed, the key to resolving the problems of nationalism and chaos in South-East Asia. But a possible Russian initiative in reviving Maphilindo might have to await the end of the Soekarno and Tengku eras in Indonesia and Malaysia.

42

In Indonesia today, students represent not merely a new generation but a new era. It is the era of greater freedom of thought and action. In academic circles in Djakarta, the atmosphere is reminiscent of the beginning of the de-Stalinization phase in Europe. There is exaggerated hope for the future, a thrill in having survived the confining years of the past.

Who are these students who have been instrumental in giving a new orientation to Indonesia's thinking and politics? In a country known for its ingenuity in coining acronyms, they call them the 66 Generation—as opposed to the generation of 1945 with their now soiled past. Student leaders disclaim responsibility for the title with a trace of exaggerated modesty. They say they are there to do the people's will, not to win glory for themselves.

The KAMI Students' Action Front has set up its headquarters in the former Chinese Consulate-General in Djakarta, ransacked by students in April. The twisted iron gates are shut and a side door is guarded by groups of students. Visitors must sign a register before entering. A student leader is addressing a large group inside, his speech punctuated by much clapping. Around the courtyard, where soldiers take a benign interest in the goings-on, other students sit in rooms, containing only bare door-frames, to discuss their affairs.

Mr Cosmas Batubara, KAMI's General Chairman, divides his time between the Consulate-General and the headquarters of his own Catholic Students' Movement, the PMKRI. A glamourized painting of General Suharto, the present Defence Minister and effective ruler, is hung beneath President Soekarno's portrait in the hall. Mr Batubara is a youthful, modest-looking man reading for a master's degree in journalism, but he wants to be a full-time politician.

Groups of students sit chatting in the hall of the PMKRI, bursts of laughter punctuating their chatter—Indonesians are basically a happy people. Others, some in their KAMI tunics, just sit and stare into blank space, as if waiting for something to happen. Mr Batubara leads me to a corner, asking an interpreter to join us. He understands English but is not a fluent English speaker.

The questions come from me in a steady stream. What are KAMI's main objectives at present ? Do you want to return to the Constitution of 1945, largely negated by President Soekarno through decrees and political manoeuvres? Do you want general elections? How do you view the postponement of the Provisional Congress—a postponement accepted with reservations by KAMI? What is your attitude to President Soekarno, Generals Suharto and Nasution, to Dr Hatta, the former Vice-President who has re-emerged on the political scene? How do you view the future of Indonesia? How do you view the mass killings following the abortive coup?

Mr Batubara answered some questions readily, others with deliberation. To some he gave evasive replies. He viewed KAMI's main objective as the ending of the Indonesian Communist Party, which was still trying to gather its badly mauled remnants. KAMI was doing this by informing the people about the PKI with the aim of "pushing it to a corner and crushing it". A team of more than 600 students is helping peasants with their crops in West Java and at the same time telling them how they had been misled in the past. KAMI's immediate objective however is to consolidate itself in the cities and a team is touring Java, Bali and other areas to gather information.

"We want to go back to the Constitution of 1945", Mr Batubara declared with emphasis. "We want to base Indonesia's policies on Panch Sheel." The Indonesian Panch Sheel is a five-point national objective which includes belief in God. He did not think general elections would be held in the country before two or three years. He warned in this context of the possibility of PKI elements re-emerging. Elections are not the main objective of his organization.

"Soekarno," Mr Batubara said, is still our President. His powers should be based on law. . . . As long as General Suharto bases his leadership on our three demands (reshuffle of the old Cabinet, banning of the PKI and the bringing down of prices) we support him. He has done a good job until now. . . . So far General Nasution has joined our demands to fight for us. He is one of the victims of the PKI coup."

About Dr Hatta, Mr Batubara was more guarded, less enthusiastic. "As long as anybody is struggling with us, we accept him. But we don't idolize anybody."

Mr Batubara, in common with most Indonesians I have talked to, viewed Indonesia's future in rosy hues. His concept of the future is an era in which the 1945 Constitution would be restored, the PKI entirely eliminated and KAMI's three demands fulfilled. "KAMI members," he pointed out, "are the young generation. They have political consciousness. They are rational and critical. They are not yes-men." The last remark was a swipe at President Soekarno's previous chief advisers.

It was hardly surprising that Mr Batubara could not fully explain the motivations of the students' upsurge. "It is the tradition of students everywhere in the world to fight for justice," he said. He averred that even before the abortive coup of October last year his Catholic Students' Movement was fighting the Communists, although this was not publicized. "We use the thirtieth September affair as a pretext to beat the PKI. People support us."

Other students, who had by this time joined our dialogue, gave me the benefit of their views. "We were ourselves surprised by our ability to do things," said one trying to explain the origins of KAMI and its phenomenal success. "Our parents were of course surprised in the beginning. They saw the danger we were in—that we might get shot. But they supported us and helped us with food and materials."

Mr Batubara, himself a Roman Catholic, ended in a Christian strain. "We are proud to be members of this generation. We don't call ourselves the 66 Generation. We are not using this name. We are young. We have many faults. Who can say what will happen in five years if we are proud of being called the 66 Generation? As people who believe in God, we believe humans are prone to make mistakes. We are mortals."

This portrait of a KAMI leader leaves many questions unanswered. A distinguished professor at the university in Djakarta suggested to me that the students revolted against the past because they simply could not live—with galloping inflation sapping their ability to make ends meet. The abandon of youth made them careless of consequences whereas the older generation, though long suffering and in dire straits, thought of the repression they would face if they dissented.

Once the students were out in the streets, they learnt that the Army, for its own interests, would protect them. And once the floodgates to dissent were opened, first by the KAMI university students and later by KAPPI secondary school students, the older generation, though shocked, grasped the opportunity and followed. President Soekarno's Tjakrabirawa guards, now disbanded, gave the students their martyr during a demonstration and his funeral in Djakarta galvanized a whole population who followed their neighbours to pay their tributes.

The winds of change blowing through Indonesia following the abortive coup and the Army's clever strategy in making use of it thus produced the spark that ignited the students' rebellion. Liberal professors in the university in Djakarta welcomed the change with open arms; some of them indeed acted as the students' advisers whose ranks also include Roman Catholic priests of Dutch descent but Indonesian nationality.

The students' revolt has already produced a dramatic change in the climate of opinion. There is a new impatience with flamboyance and histrionics. It is the fashion now to decry prestige projects and wasteful expenditure. "Yes-men" has become a dirty phrase. And the Government has seen it fit to encourage a week-long seminar at the university in Djakarta whose upshot was a sharp cry for a return to the rule of law.

On the obverse side, it is somewhat frightening for an observer of the Indonesian scene returning to the country to find new ideas already being used as catch phrases and slogans. To a nation fed on cliches for years, acronyms and slogans come naturally. GESTAPU, the acronym to describe and condemn the abortive coup, was a brilliant piece of political propaganda. But now there is the 66 Generation, AMPERA, denoting the suffering of the people, and even the call for a return to the 1945 Constitution has become something of a slogan.

What of the future? There are complaints that students are being used by interested parties for their personal ends. In universities, professors are being sacked for their alleged pro-Communist tendencies although some might have had no connection with the coup. The students, having once tasted power, will be loath to let it go and many students will find the life of bending events to their desires more interesting than the somewhat mundane business of attending classes. Student attendance in universities is still very poor.

Largely by circumstances but also through courage, students have thus become a political factor of consequence. KAMI delegations regularly meet the generals and no major political decision is taken without the students being consulted and their acquiescence, if not enthusiasm, secured. President Soekarno's action in revamping his Supreme Advisory Council brought forth a storm of protest and its indefinite postponement.

Although KAMI and the other student groups have proved to be of invaluable help to the Army in consolidating its power, the future might see a parting of the ways. General Suharto's strategy is to evoke a consensus in the country in dealing with President Soekarno. The pace is necessarily slow, while students are traditionally impetuous. Besides, the intolerable economic plight of most city dwellers —an essential ingredient in the students' revolt—might prove too much of a task for the Army and its supporters. A new crisis in the economic or political field might see new fireworks.

43

It has become customary to compare Indonesian developments with the old but still living art of the Indonesian puppet play. There are so many shadowy aspects of the internal power play, so many loose ends to be tied, so much prevarication that it is tempting to take shelter behind allegorical symbols.

This habit is not confined to foreign commentators in search of a definition of Indonesian developments. Many Javanese in the entourage of the present rulers themselves describe events as having reached the two a.m. stage of the puppet play, which usually lasts well into the early hours of the morning.

Yet, in spite of the admittedly fluid situation, one can assess the trends and personalities of Indonesia today. In spite of the future being clouded over with uncertainties of circumstance and temperament, one can draw certain conclusions. First, is the trend set in motion by the ill-fated coup attempt of October 1 last year irreversible? It is irreversible in the sense that it has brought forth a surge of new feelings and expectations, crystallized new pressure groups and given the Army a primacy it will do its best to retain. It is reversible to the extent that the Indonesian Communist Party will re-emerge in the future; Indonesian foreign policy aims of claiming a primacy at the expense of the British and subsequently American military presence in the area will re-emerge, perhaps with less flamboyance.

What the ruling triumvirate, consisting of General Suharto, the Sultan of Jogjakarta and Dr Adam Malik, is trying to do represents both a short-term and a long-term exercise. The two are, of course, inter-related but the immediate aspects of present Indonesian efforts are more dramatic in character, not because they represent revolutionary concepts but because they are a revolutionary departure from the past.

It is axiomatic that the foreign policy aims of a country have to be related to domestic needs. Yet President Soekarno and his chief advisers had strayed so far from the path of reality that they left the present regime with a foreign debt of US $ 2.4 billion, a hydra-headed inflation, no industrial base to speak of and a variety of incomplete prestigious monuments.

The new regime's first action was to acknowledge the desperateness of the situation. Then it set about seeking deferment of foreign debts and the inflow of new aid. Both these problems are not insurmountable although the latter will depend upon the political stability that is achieved at home. The internal economic situation is more intractable because of the fantastic inflation prevalent in the country and all its attendant ills.

There are already murmurs in Djakarta that the Sultan of Jogjakarta, who is in charge of the Herculean economic task, is not moving fast enough. The Sultan's immediate success is obviously dependent upon the amount of political stability the triumvirate can achieve, but even in making the beginnings of a new economic policy there seems to be a drag. The Sultan is a pleasant and respected Javanese leader but he has still to prove his capacity for taking and implementing ruthless decisions the situation demands.

In the foreign policy field, the triumvirate's actions represent the Army's basic anti-Communist character at home and its desire to consolidate its power by bringing about a certain amount of economic stability. The new regime's desire to bring an expensive and senseless confrontation of Malaysia to an end is thus a recognition of its past failure and the need to stop a fruitless drain of money and prestige. Obviously, the extent of foreign aid Indonesia receives in the future will depend upon the Army's success in reversing the confrontation policy and achieving stability at home.

In keeping with the Army's desire to detach the country from its former increasing dependence on China, Indonesia's new policy is to maintain a more non-aligned posture. Dr Adam Malik's inclusion in the ruling triumvirate was a recognition of the need to have a Left-wing symbol as also a tribute to his considerable diplomatic and intellectual capacities. But Dr Malik, in spite of his revolutionary past, has no political base; his small Murba Party is still technically banned.

Indeed, Dr Malik is the most controversial of the three members of the triumvirate. Some leaders of the Nahdatul Ulama, the largest political party today, make no secret of their distrust of a person they describe as a "fellow traveller". Dr Malik's usefulness to the Army, particularly to General Suharto, in projecting and implementing new policies is, however, recognized and although his status might be scaled down in a new Cabinet, it seems unlikely that he will lose stewardship of the Foreign Office.

General Suharto has emerged as a major leader although he was an almost unknown soldier before last October's coup attempt. A Javanese, like President Soekarno, he is inclined to move slowly but, in spite of his mild exterior, he has displayed a strong will in tackling crisis situations. Although General Suharto is not enamoured of elections as a panacea for all ills, he would rather keep the Army as the power behind the throne than run the country through a military junta.

The relationship between General Suharto and General Nasution is intriguing. The latter has been very vocal in spite of the fact that he has not particularly distinguished himself in times of crises in the past. Today he stands on the fringe of power, his only official position being that of Deputy Commander of the Crush Malaysia Command. There are reportedly differences between the two Generals on forcing the pace of political developments; General Nasution is ironically considered a "hawk" in the new situation. There is little doubt, however, that he still enjoys respect as a senior soldier and may be called upon to fill a presidential or vice-presidential position.

In pursuing the new policies, General Suharto and his two colleagues in the triumvirate are facing several kinds and degrees of pressures. The most formidable opponent of the new regime is President Soekarno, whose power lies in his capacity for negative action and his lingering but considerable hold over Central and East Java. To many members of the Armed Forces and political parties as well, Dr Soekarno still represents a cherished symbol.

In Djakarta, on the other hand, the emasculation of the President's powers is strikingly brought home. Days, and sometimes weeks, go by without his making a single speech. He is denied the use of the radio to broadcast to the people and his visitors must pass Army scrutiny. His telephone calls are monitored and, with the disbandment of his Tjakrabirawa guards, his security is directly supervised by the Army.

General Suharto and his colleagues would best like Dr Soekarno to remain a figurehead President; although he represents a symbol of the past, it is a symbol the triumvirate still needs to avoid dissension within the Armed Forces and the country. Dr Soekarno has not accepted the role the Army would have him play and a last card he can use is to move Indonesia's capital to Jogjakarta where his image remains largely untarnished.

Two other kinds of pressure the new regime faces come from student groups, now called the '66 Generation, and the political parties. The students' demands are largely idealistic but no less pressing for that. They have enunciated their more immediate aims by demanding an early session of the Provisional Congress and the formation of a new Cabinet. There are many politicians who are looking upon the KAMI and KAPPI student groups as a potential source of support. So far the students have resisted giving block support to any individual or political party; their loyalty to the Army is laced with a continuing desire to assess its actions critically. Clearly, the students represent a limiting factor in the Army's strategy.

The political parties are a different kind of pressure for the Army. The great burst of activity within the parties demonstrates their desire to secure as large a slice of the cake of power as they can. For parties like the Nahdatul Ulama, basking in the glow of the post-coup decimation of the PKI, the future looks rosy. But the NU is a very amorphous party and faces some competition from the Muhamadijah, a social organization which wants to adopt a political garb, and the Masjumi, technically banned but in the process of surfacing again.

The Nationalist Party, the PNI, is split down the middle by the recent acquisition of power by the moderate wing;

the left-wing Ali Sastroamidjojo group, which lost out in the power struggle following the coup, still exercises some influence. There is talk in Djakarta of a group of Leftist parties like the Murba and the old Socialist Party, the PSI, banding together to form a league. In spite of General Suharto's denial that a new socialist party is essential to the country's immediate needs, there are indications that he would welcome its formation.

Essentially, the Army wants to take over President Soekarno's former role of balancing the various political factions to maintain power. Suggestions that the Army itself should become something of a political party are resisted because General Suharto wants to remain above the din of political squabbles to be able to direct the course of events. He would be reluctant to give the NU too large a share of the cake for the same reasons.

In spite of the present persistent demands for a return to the Constitution of 1945, the future governmental structure has yet to be determined. The '45 Constitution envisages a strong President acting within a legal framework, but questions such as the proportion of elective legislators and the precise extent of Armed Forces' representation have yet to be settled.

A blueprint for Indonesia of the future will emerge after the results of the present power play have crystallized. To an extent, the Army can threaten to rule as a junta to bring the political parties into line.

44

Malaysia is living in a state of suspended animation. The Bangkok peace talks with Indonesia held early in June are being presented as the end of confrontation and Tun

Abdul Razak, Malaysia's Deputy Prime Minister and chief negotiator, is being feted in various towns for his success in striking peace with Indonesia.

There is, indeed, some welcome evidence of change. Radio Djakarta has stopped broadcasting Crush Malaysia slogans even as Indonesian spokesmen report meetings of the Crush Malaysia Command with a straight face. The Malaysian radio plays requests sent in by Indonesians and popular Indonesian songs, once banned, again hold sway over the air.

There is talk too of reviving the old and eminently sensible proposal of bringing uniformity to the Malay and Indonesian languages. The prospect of peace with Indonesia has released the bottled-up feelings of the Malays of Malaysia for their "blood brothers" in Indonesia. This has caused a measure of nervousness among the Chinese, and Malaysian leaders have been quick to condemn foreign Powers for their allegedly dubious motives, darkly hinting at Britain.

Lately, however, Malaysian leaders have had to break it gently to their people that they must give the Indonesians some time to change. The truth of the matter is that while the Bangkok talks have opened the path to peace and the trend of recent Indonesian policy is particularly helpful, the restoration of diplomatic relations between the two countries is likely to take several months, and possibly longer.

Two factors are responsible for this setback to Malaysian leaders' initial hopes. The formal ending of confrontation has become involved in the final act of Indonesia's internal problem of confining President Soekarno to a strict regimen of rules and regulations. Second, the peace formula worked out on the Malaysian Borneo States is being interpreted differently by the two sides.

At Bangkok, Tun Razak gave an assurance to Indonesia's brilliant Foreign Minister, Dr Adam Malik, that Malaysia would wait patiently while he and his Army colleagues sold the peace plan in Djakarta. Although Malaysians were thus aware of Dr Malik's problems, they perhaps did not fully anticipate the complexities of the Indonesian political scene.

Central to these complexities is the fact that unless President Soekarno gives his approval to the ending of confrontation, General Suharto and his colleagues must use the indirect and time-consuming methods of Indonesian politics to achieve their goal. Since there are differences within the Indonesian Army and between the Army and the political parties on the larger question of the structure and personnel of Government in a post-Soekarno Indonesia, the final settlement with Malaysia might have to wait its turn.

Malaysian leaders continue to believe that General Suharto and Dr Malik have both the will and the capacity to see the Bangkok agreement through. They are particularly pinning their hopes on an Indonesian liaison team setting up shop in Kuala Lumpur soon to resolve the immediate problems of peace as and when they arise. If a semi-permanent Malaysian team also goes to Djakarta, a valuable two-way contact would be established.

Essentially, the Borneo peace formula, still to be ratified by the Indonesian Government, is a rather straightforward document. It envisages general elections in the two Malaysian Borneo States through which the people would be afforded an opportunity to reaffirm their desire to remain in Malaysia. No date is set for the elections nor does the formula specifically make Indonesian recognition of Malaysia dependent upon them.

The Malaysian interpretation of the formula seems to be that elections in the two Malaysian Borneo States would be held as and when feasible and that Indonesia would accord full diplomatic recognition to Malaysia almost immediately after the peace formula is ratified by its Government. If this interpretation is accurate, Malaysia's negotiators at Bangkok have scored a significant victory.

However, even during the last day of the Bangkok peace talks, it became apparent that Indonesians were giving a different interpretation to the formula. They were implying that Indonesian recognition of Malaysia would follow—not precede—elections in the States of Sabah and Sarawak. On the other hand, Malaysians plainly rejected Indonesian demands for a referendum in the Borneo States and it was because of Indonesia's need for a *de facto* settlement with Malaysia that prompted Dr Malik to accept a watered down formula.

Indonesians are now suggesting that while it is up to Malaysia to fix a date for elections in Sabah and Sarawak, Djakarta will not extend diplomatic recognition to Kuala Lumpur until they are held. If Indonesians pursue such a course of action, it will come as a disappointment to the Malaysians. Elections in Sabah could be held by the end of the year, but general elections in the more sensitive State of Sarawak are not due for a considerable time yet.

There is, on the other hand, little doubt that the trend of Indonesian policy is towards making peace with Malaysia. The ending of confrontation in practice, if not in form, is obviously essential to Indonesia attracting significant foreign aid to set its economic house in order. But Indonesians are still not averse to extracting a higher price than Malaysia is prepared to pay for the formal ending of confrontation. Malaysian leaders are somewhat at a disadvantage in dealing with Indonesian tactics because they have prematurely announced the end of confrontation. Besides, Djakarta can use the continuing rivalry between Singapore and Kuala Lumpur to its own advantage.

Although Tengku Abdul Rahman has welcomed Indonesia's recognition of Singapore, it came as something of a surprise to Kuala Lumpur that Djakarta would extend its recognition as quickly as it did. Kuala Lumpur chose to interpret this step as a good augury for an early diplomatic recognition of Malaysia, an interpretation that is likely to be proved wrong.

For the present, Singapore's Prime Minister feels impelled to play his hand modestly, probably because he feels that with a rapprochement between Indonesia and Malaysia in the offing, he has less room for manoeuvre. He has publicly declared that he will not exchange diplomatic representatives with Indonesia till Malaysia is in a position to do so. But this will not prevent Singapore permitting Indonesian trade representatives to be stationed on the island before Kuala Lumpur has a chance to get off the mark in trading with Indonesia.

The last act of the ending of confrontation is thus likely to contain some tortuous scenes. And until confrontation is finally buried with due ceremony, talk about a grand alliance of regional co-operation will have an unreal quality about it. Burma seems to have fewer reservations than it did about joining an expanded Association of South-East Asia now comprising Malaysia, Thailand and the Philippines. But Indonesia's projected inclusion in such a grouping is likely to raise questions about the organization's political motives. Besides, there is the unresolved problem of Singapore's place in it. It is, however, a striking indication of the changed climate in Indonesia and Malaysia that thoughts should now turn to regional co-operation rather than confrontation.

45

Singapore celebrates the first anniversary of its separate independence in a confident mood, in sharp contrast to

Mr Lee Kuan Yew's tears which heralded the city State's birth a year ago. This confidence does not spring from complacency about troubles that lie ahead, but from a belief that the State has reason to be satisfied with its achievements of the past year.

The first six months' confusion has gradually given way to a more sober assessment of the tiny Republic's place and problems. Headline-catching disclosures from musty files on CIA agents and sabre rattling with Malaysia have been replaced for the moment by more pertinent thoughts and actions.

Mr Lee Kuan Yew and his colleagues have demonstrated that, in the short run, they can adapt their policies to new circumstances and their country's interests. At the core of these interests lies the State's economic viability, and it is because of the leaders' belief that they have crossed the initial hurdle that they radiate a measure of confidence and appear more relaxed.

Singapore accomplished its immediate economic survival through a two-pronged drive. First, the Republic linked the defence interests of the Western countries and Australia and New Zealand with the necessity of keeping Singapore afloat economically. Second, it set about winning friends in the Soviet Union and other East European countries.

To begin with, Singapore's aggressive salesmanship in demanding that a percentage of its goods must receive the right of entry into Britain, Australia, New Zealand and the USA because the island was the bastion of Western defence interests in South-East Asia proved unproductive. Mr Lee's style of diplomacy was resented in many Western countries as also his exaggerated notions about the importance of the Singapore base.

While Australia and New Zealand, feeling more vulnerable and therefore dependent upon the Singapore base, did not take issue with Mr Lee about his implied threats, others did. In London in April, it was made quite clear to Mr Lee that since the British base was already subsidizing Singapore's economy to the tune of about 25%, it would be unrealistic of him to expect further large-scale economic assistance. Mr Lee did not press his point.

Mr Lee tried to apply pressure on the USA by refusing to raise the status of the American Consulate-General to that of an Embassy although an Ambassador-designate was reportedly cooling his heels in Washington for months. Singapore made exaggerated demand on the USA for a quota on cotton textiles—only to be met with a polite but firm refusal. The American attitude was that while it wished to do its bit for the island's economic welfare, it would not be blackmailed. Finally, Singapore scaled down its demand from about 100 million square yards to 35 million. The US Consulate-General was raised to the level of an Embassy nearly eight months after Singapore became independent.

Singapore thus learned to temper its aggressiveness in putting across its point of view. Most Western nations with a direct interest in the island's stability, on their part, conceded that they should help in keeping Singapore a viable entity.

Mr Lee undertook an extensive tour of Russia and other East European countries in May. His objective was economic and political. Economically, Singapore wanted to tap East Europe for trade; politically, Mr Lee wished to reduce his vulnerability to Leftist criticism by emphasizing the temporary nature of the base and the argument that there was no immediate alternative for safeguarding the island's security. He succeeded in achieving both his objectives.

The Soviet Union was particularly interested in obtaining a new window on South-East Asia and Moscow as well as other European Communist capitals wanted to promote direct trade, specially for purchases of Malaysian rubber. In consequence, the *New Times* of Moscow wrote a highly flattering article on Singapore. Tass has established an office on the island and a Russian trade mission is being set up. Bulgaria has already opened a trade office while trade agreements have been signed with Russia, Poland and Bulgaria.

Singapore is eagerly looking forward to resuming normal trade with Indonesia after three years of confrontation. The first phase of discussions between the two countries has been completed and it is hoped that the Singapore-Indonesia trade will touch the 40% mark of the pre-confrontation level. This will, no doubt, prove highly profitable to the skilled entrepot merchants of the island State.

While these developments have naturally heartened the people of Singapore, relations with Malaysia and the future shape of things in the region remain at the heart of the island's basic problems. Mr Lee and his colleagues have been exercising restraint in exchanging polemics with Malaysian leaders during the last few months. Notwithstanding this welcome change, sniping at Malaysia's values and achievements continues from the Singapore end, not to speak of the fire-breathing exercises in Malaysia.

There are three basic problems between Singapore and Malaysia. First, Mr Lee's personality and style of doing things arouses instant hostility in Malaysia. Second, the Singapore leaders must convince Malaysians that they are concerned only with their new nation's prosperity and progress and not with reforming or changing Malaysia's political mores; hence they must renounce visions of reunification. The third, most important, problem is that Singapore is a Chinese city State and Malaysia is politically a Malay-dominated country.

Singapore is very conscious of the third problem and is not unaware of the pulls that will come into play once

Malaysia and Indonesia patch up their quarrels. It is ironic that Mr Lee's great advocacy of equal rights for the Chinese in Malaysia has only served to heighten Malays' suspicions and their desire to have very close relations with Indonesians. Since Malays own and operate little wealth in Malaysia, it seems inevitable that they will ultimately seek their salvation in a union or alliance with Indonesia; the Indonesian desire to resume normal trade with Singapore is a short-term exercise because of Djakarta's dire economic needs.

Singapore's much vaunted policy of multi-racialism and multi-linguism suits Mr Lee as long as he can interest Western nations in his survival. Besides, he has not given up all hopes of a return to a union with Malaya (the two Malaysian Borneo States are a somewhat impermanent adjunct) some time in the future. Mr Lee has at the same time been throwing out hints about the island's "other alternatives". One of these alternatives is a Chinese Singapore becoming a "third China". Singapore has a window on China through Cambodia with which it is maintaining close relations, and Peking has so far refrained from making a single disparaging remark about independent Singapore or its leaders.

The retention of the British base is central to Mr Lee's strategy for the immediate future. Apart from its economic benefits, it is an insurance against a two-pronged Malay-Indonesian drive to whittle down a Chinese Singapore. This is one of the many reasons why Britain might not want to stay on in Singapore for too long. Apart from the basic problems of maintaining Britain's East-of-Suez posture, London would be in a particularly unhappy position in seeking to protect Chinese interests in a largely Malay world.

The interesting transformation of Mr Lee's views about the Vietnam war must be ascribed to his worries about the base (he now believes Britain will maintain the Singapore base for the next five years). Mr Lee has lately been showing a sympathetic appreciation of the US role in Vietnam and has related the American presence there to the time being "bought" by Singapore to consolidate its independence through industrialization and efficient trading. Perhaps Mr Lee's new understanding of American policy also springs from the fact that Washington has been largely responsible for persuading Britain not to run down the Singapore base a year after Indonesian confrontation would end, as was originally planned.

There are good reasons to temper the official mood of confidence about Singapore's future with reservations. For while Singapore likes to think of itself as a pivot of South-East Asia, it is a very troubled world it lives in, apart from its congenital problems of relations with Malaysia and the problems created by the island's own mood and politicians. It has, for instance, been suggested by some members of the United Malays National Organization in the neighbouring State of Johore that the causeway linking Singapore with Malaya should be blown up.

Meanwhile, Mr Lee rules the island with his own brand of democratic socialism; neither democracy nor socialism is an immutable attribute for him. Indeed, Singapore resembles a one-party State more than a parliamentary democracy. Mr Lee has been so efficient in reducing the opposition to impotency (he received help from the opposition leaders' own foolish tactics) that his People's Action Party reigns supreme. The opposition Barisan Socialists, who still call Singapore's independence "phoney", have had the somewhat sardonic pleasure of highlighting Mr Lee's inclinations towards a one-party State by boycotting parliamentary sittings since independence.

Ironically, Singapore Government spokesmen themselves have had to remind the world recently that the

Communist danger is not over. Credible local Communist opposition is sometimes a valuable commodity. On the other hand, an impressive queue of ex-detainees appears on television from time to time. Their refrain, which helped to obtain their release, is constant: they were mistaken in turning to Communism to solve Singapore's problems. The former political prisoners have formed their own Welfare Association, apparently with official encouragement.

46

Kuala Lumpur wore a big smile on August 12 to welcome the Indonesian Foreign Minister, Dr Adam Malik, and his party of 50, who arrived there on a one-day visit which marks the beginning of friendly relations between the two countries.

To people in Kuala Lumpur, particularly the Malays, the occasion had many emotional overtones. The Indonesian national anthem was played during the airport ceremonies—the first time in Malaysia since confrontation began three years ago. The Indonesian flag was given pride of place beside the Malaysian flag and the drum beats and the guard of honour all signified a new phase in the two countries' relations.

Dr Malik and the Malaysian Deputy Premier, Tun Abdul Razak, who had himself arrived from Djakarta just before the Indonesians after signing the peace agreement, later met the Press to add little to the world's knowledge of events, but they exuded happiness and confidence in the future. Tun Razak announced that a Malaysian had just taken over command of military forces in the two Borneo States—signifying the projected withdrawal of British troops from Eastern Malaysia.

While Malaysians have the right to feel pleased about the signing of the agreement in Djakarta and over Dr Malik's goodwill visit, the problems of implementing the agreement will soon loom large. It seems that Indonesia will take some time to establish formal diplomatic relations by the exchange of fully accredited envoys. Although this question is not formally linked to the holding of general elections in the Borneo States, it is so linked in many Indonesians' minds. Besides, the speed with which the agreement will be implemented will depend upon Indonesia's internal problems.

For its part, Malaysia now seems more inclined to have early general elections in the Borneo States to fulfil one aspect of the agreement. Indonesians have agreed that a verdict of the Borneo people in favour of Malaysia at the time of elections will satisfy them.

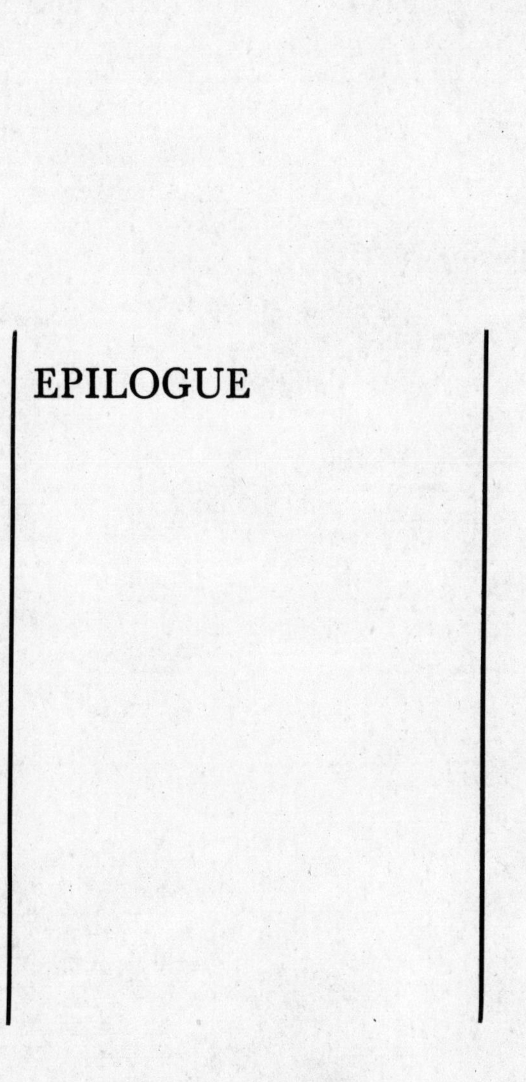

EPILOGUE

Looking at the Malaysian world from the vantage point of May, 1970, some of the old cries seem remote. Yet events in the intervening years have merely served to highlight the relevance of Maphilindo to Malaysia, Indonesia and the Philippines. The basic problem of Malaysia—the mixed racial complexion of its population—stands out in bold relief.

To anyone familiar with the story of Malaysia, the race riots in Malaya in May, 1969—deplorable as they were—would not have come as a surprise. Against the backdrop of the classical ingredients of racial conflict, UMNO's performance in the general election in 1969 was a signal for Malay revolt. Tengku Abdul Rahman's party lost votes to the Right and the Left—to the Malay-based PMIP and the Chinese-dominated Democratic Action Party.

This produced two kinds of reaction among Malays. The first was the realization that UMNO's somewhat centrist approach had failed to keep many Malay voters with it. Secondly, Malays felt that the Chinese and Indians had forfeited their privileges on Malay soil by repudiating the communal parties allied to UMNO in the Alliance Government.

The formation of the National Operations Council under Tun Abdul Razak's chairmanship was more than a law and order measure to control the communal carnage. It was a temporary expedient to project the nation's Malay leadership into a more purposeful role in relation to improving the lot of Malays. Inevitably, one of the first measures of the Council was to tighten employment and citizenship laws.

A year after the race riots, Malaysia continues to be subjected to emergency regulations. The National Operations Council is becoming a rather permanent feature of life, but the scheme under which short-term permits were given to non-citizens, many of whom had been reared in Malaysia, was not a success. Malays did not take up jobs that were theirs for the asking on rubber plantations.

The reorientation of Malays, whose lives often centre round their *kampongs* and smallholdings, is a long-term problem. Meanwhile, Malaysia must live. The Chinese have been associated with the emergency Government in a subsidiary capacity. Short-term permit holders have been promised an extension if no Malays come forward to take their jobs.

Yet Malaysia cannot go back to the somnolent pre-Malaysia phase. Mr Lee Kuan Yew's turbulent entry into Malaysian politics had destroyed the comfortable basis on which Malaya had continued to prosper and live in peace—a clean division of political and economic power between Malays and Chinese. The young Chinese, in any event, was not prepared to accept his father's thesis of paying obeisance to the Malay in order to prosper. The young Malay, on the other hand, either espoused the PMIP line in wanting to pull his fellow Malays out of poverty or was attracted to Left-leaning parties to break the union, as he saw it, between the feudal Malays and rich Chinese merchants.

Recent student demands in Malaya for Tengku Abdul Rahman's retirement are one indication of the new urges among young Malays. And the Tengku's decision to sack a young Malay Minister, Mr Musa Hitam, for his alleged extremist views is another straw in the wind. I have had the privilege of knowing Mr Hitam. He is no extremist, but a leader devoted to the cause of the uplift of Malays and fired by the concept of a pan-Malay movement, whose attraction for Malay intellectuals is beyond dispute.

It is no coincidence that the race riots and the tensions between Malays and Chinese (Indians are a subsidiary problem) that have come to the surface were followed by a new offensive by Communist guerrillas harbouring in the border areas of Malaya and Thailand. The Communist insurgency that spilled over into Malaya's first years of independence was licked by the identification of Communists with the Chinese. With many Chinese dissatisfied with the scheme of things in Malaysia, the Peking-directed guerrillas felt the time was propitious to hot up things again along the jungle borders. And they are encouraging dissension in the Muslim Southern Thai States.

Malaysia's concern over the resurgence of guerrilla activity is reflected in its spiralling defence Budget. For the first time, Malaysia's defence and internal security requirements took precedence over social services. In the Malaysian Budget for 1970-71, expenditure on defence is of the order of M$ 535 million and internal security claims M$ 268 million. To be sure, Malaysia also has an insurgency problem at its other extremity, the Sarawak jungles bordering on Indonesia. However, it has the good fortune of receiving the co-operation of its two neighbouring States in fighting the insurgents, although at one time Kuala Lumpur felt the Thais could be more energetic.

But Malaysia's greatest asset is its continuing prosperity. In spite of the month-long race riots of 1969 and their impact on commerce and industry, Malaysia finished up with peak foreign exchange reserves. The State's two main products, rubber and tin, enjoyed a good price on the world market and its relatively new interest in palm oil yielded rich dividends. These factors, coupled with a high level of Government spending, created boom conditions. These conditions could change if Malaysia's two primary products dip low on the world market.

* * *

It is ironic that Mr Lee Kuan Yew, who took Singapore into Malaysia on the plea that the State could not exist as a separate independent entity, has spent the last few years disproving his own thesis. The impressive strides the State has made in paying its way in a competitive world is a tribute to Mr Lee's pragmatism and Singapore's hard working population.

Singapore's last Budget reflected near boom conditions. Two factors were largely responsible for the State's prosperity: its success in exploiting its geographic location and the rush for off-shore oil exploration in the region. Mr Lee realizes very well that only by an all-out industrialization programme could the wolf be kept away from Singapore's door, and he has acted upon his realization.

New industries are mushrooming all over the State, an Esso refinery is being built and the British naval base has been converted into a shipyard. The departure of British troops by the end of 1971 is not merely a security problem for Singapore, but also an economic problem.

As long as Mr Lee's Government can provide a booming economy and a shortening unemployment roll, he, and the State, are all right. But Singapore lives in a dangerous world, in recognition of which the State's defence Budget has soared to 31.7% of its national Budget. Mr Lee has decided on a citizen's army and a midget air force to serve as deterrents.

In spite of the Foreign Minister's denial of Singapore being an Israel in South-East Asia, there is a natural inclination to turn to Israel and draw inspiration from it, particularly in the military field. Twenty-three Israeli experts are reported to be working in Singapore to train the State's army.

But next only to its economic viability, Singapore's problems are political. The Malaysia experience rankles on both sides of the causeway. Singapore's influence on the elections in Malaya in 1969 was naturally not to UMNO's liking. The race riots spilled over into Singapore although they were quickly controlled.

With its other Malay neighbour, Indonesia, Singapore has been having its problems. In October, 1968, the Singapore Embassy in Djakarta was sacked following the execution of two Indonesians pronounced guilty for their acts of sabotage on the island during the "confrontation" phase. Clemency pleas by Indonesia and Malaysia failed to avert the execution.

Singapore's relations with Indonesia are on a more even keel today, but the explosive Malay-Chinese confrontation in Malaysia and, to a lesser extent, Indonesia poses immediate and inevitable problems for the State. Mr Lee has learnt to trim his sails to concentrate on the State's economic and industrialization problems. In this lies Singapore's hope for the future.

Mr Lee's system of government continues to be untrammelled by the finer points of parliamentary democracy. But in some ways, his biggest political coup in recent years has been the "reform" in prison of his once formidable rival, Mr Lim Chin Siong, and his subsequent release.

* * *

Indonesia is taking the hard road to economic solvency. It is a long road. But fiscal discipline has been rewarded by rather generous foreign aid in today's context and inflation, that bane of Indonesian economy, has been kept in check. Indonesia is still saddled with the problem of the rescheduling of its old debts. Its Western creditors have proved to be more understanding than the Soviet Union. Out of a total estimated debt of $ 2,202.5 million, Russia's share is $ 696.6 million.

Indonesia's present phase of economic and industrial rehabilitation has been set in motion by a five-year plan, launched in April, 1969. Western investors are back in the field, apart from the tenacious Japanese, and a number of joint collaboration agreements have been signed for offshore oil prospecting and rehabilitating industries.

President Suharto's dilemma is that political problems are again coming to the fore and could crowd out the economic priorities. The nature of these problems are revealing. Nearly five years after the abortive coup and Dr Soekarno's downfall, senior armed forces' officers are still being weeded out for their alleged pro-Soekarno tendencies and involvement in the coup. About 350 detention camps and rehabilitation centres hold over 75,000 prisoners—those arrested after the coup, although some other groups have been let off after indoctrination.

Budget spending on the armed forces, which was as high as 70% during Dr Soekarno's "confrontation" phase, has been substantially reduced. But the armed forces have not been found wanting in generating funds for their needs, through their business enterprises or other less acceptable methods. Students have again raised their voice against corruption in the armed forces; President Suharto's response has been to appoint a "Committee of Four".

The armed forces have traditionally faced strains from within. Not all the officers arrested or retired from service were implicated in the coup; at least some of them had political ambitions. In October, 1969, President Suharto undertook a drastic reorganization with the object of strengthening his position by replacing the service chiefs and restricting their powers. In a country in which effective power lies with the armed forces, a periodic reshuffle of senior officers and commands becomes necessary to prevent the more ambitious ones from organizing a palace coup.

General elections are now promised in July, 1971. They may or may not be held, but no one believes they will change the power structure in the country. The armed forces mean to stay in command, and it might well be argued that, faced with the dimensions of Indonesia's problems, there is no other comparable cohesive force to run the country. But the armed forces can ignore the demand for a clean Government at their cost.

In foreign policy, Indonesians have demonstrated their inborn resilience. A dialogue with the Soviet Union has begun, in spite of the debt problem and the psychological factors involved on the Soviet side. While the policy directions of President Suharto's Government are guided by the necessity of Western aid and investment and the anti-Communist slant of many senior officers, he has wisely decided not to tilt too far in one direction. And Indonesians had recovered their composure sufficiently to host an Asian conference on Cambodia in May, 1970.

Indonesia's natural affinity with Malaysia was demonstrated by the exchange of visits by Tengku Abdul Rahman and President Suharto, by the two countries' agreement to demarcate the continental shelf and the numerous delegations that have been shuttling back and forth. The agreements have ranged from exchange of television programmes to the supply of Indonesian school teachers for Malaysia. The two countries have signed a treaty of friendship and co-operation in economic, cultural and social spheres.

* * *

The Philippines' relations with Malaysia have continued to follow a zig-zag path, saddled as they are with the former's luckless claim to Sabah. Diplomatic relations between the two countries have been resumed after a long break. The claim has become a part of the Philippines' turbulent politics and is destined to raise its head from time to time.

The country's problems are economic and political, the two intertwined in its special relations with the USA. By virtue of these relations, Filipino products enjoy concessions on the U.S. market, but the reciprocal rights they entail for Americans in the Philippines are creating anti-American feelings that are threatening to sweep the country. But the Philippines must find alternative markets and renegotiate the agreement on American bases before ending these relations.

In spite of the gains recorded in agriculture, manufacturing and mining sectors, the Philippines faced a serious monetary crisis in 1969, thanks to large deficit spending by the Government and trade imbalances. The Government hopes to meet the crisis by cutting expenditure, restricting credit, raising dollar credits and practicing austerity.

President Marcos had the unusual distinction of being elected to a second term of office in November, 1969, only to be faced a few months later by unprecedented anti-Government students' demonstrations. The demands included extra funds for education, a non-partisan convention to amend the constitution and "clean and honest" elections. The President had to trim his sails by promising not to stand for a third term (the constitution permits only two terms for a President), accepting the resignation of the constabulary chief and later revamping his Cabinet.

* * *

The Association of South-East Asian Nations (ASEAN) is the only somewhat nebulous regional political organization of which Malaysia, Indonesia and the Philippines are members. Its other members are Singapore and Thailand. For Malaysia and Singapore, in particular, the problems of security loom large, with the announced departure of British troops by the end of 1971.

Australia shares the anxieties of these two countries and has made careful commitments for their security. In the defence plans envisaged so far, the Australians have made three stipulations. They are not taking over Britain's role, their interest is in the security of the Malayan peninsula (thus leaving out the disputed Sabah area) and the defence of Malaya and Singapore is indivisible.

Present arrangements envisage the stationing of Australian and New Zealand troops in Malaya and Singapore, and the integrated air defence system calls for the pooling of Australian, Malaysian and Singapore aircraft and ground facilities. After a period of initial hesitation, Australia sees itself as the most significant regional Power of the future.

Towards the Soviet Union, Malaysia and its neighbours are adopting a new "open door" policy, matched by a growing Russian interest in the Indian Ocean and South-East Asia. To an extent, the new attitude of these countries is determined by their trade interests (Russia is a major buyer of Malaysian rubber); in part, by their recognition of Russia's role as a super Power.

For Mr Lee Kuan Yew, in particular, the Soviet Union provides a second string to his bow. Careful leaks about Singapore's willingness to give Soviet naval vessels repair facilities are meant to excite Western interest in the island's future.

But Russia's new presence in South-East Asia and the defence arrangements Malaysia has with Australia are not a long-term answer to its problems. Nor can the Philippines' dependence on American bases be politically acceptable to the country for long. Only a Maphilindo grouping can provide the two countries with an adequate defence system —once Indonesia has got over its recuperative phase.

APPENDICES

1

MALAYSIA AGREEMENT

The following is the text of the agreement relating to Malaysia signed in London on July 9, 1963:

Agreement Relating to Malaysia

The United Kingdom of Great Britain and Northern Ireland, the Federation of Malaya, North Borneo, Sarawak and Singapore

Desiring to conclude an Agreement relating to Malaysia agree as follows:

Article I

The colonies of North Borneo and Sarawak and the State of Singapore shall be federated with the existing States of the Federation of Malaya, the States of Sabah, Sarawak and Singapore in accordance with the constitutional instruments annexed to this Agreement and the Federation shall thereafter be called "Malaysia".

Article II

The Government of the Federation of Malaya will take such steps as may be appropriate and available to them to secure the enactment by the Parliament of the Federation of Malaya of an Act in the form set out in Annex A to this Agreement and that it is brought into operation on 31st August, 1963 (and the date on which the said Act is brought into operation is hereinafter referred to as "Malaysia Day").

Article III

The Government of the United Kingdom will submit to Her Britannic Majesty before Malaysia Day Orders in Council for the purpose of giving the force of law to the Constitutions of Sabah, Sarawak and Singapore as States of Malaysia which are set out in Annexes B, C and D in this Agreement.

Article IV

The Government of the United Kingdom will take such steps as may be appropriate and available to them to secure the enactment by the Parliament of the United Kingdom of an Act providing for the relinquishment, as from Malaysia Day, of Her Britannic Majesty's sovereignty and jurisdiction in respect of North Borneo, Sarawak and Singapore so that the said sovereignty and jurisdiction shall on such relinquishment vest in accordance with this Agreement and the Constitutional instruments annexed to this Agreement.

Article V

The Government of the Federation of Malaya will take such steps as may be appropriate and available to them to secure the enactment before Malaysia Day by the Parliament of the Federation of Malaya of an Act in the form set out in Annex E to this Agreement for the purpose of extending and adapting the Immigration Ordinance, 1959, of the Federation of Malaya to Malaysia and making additional provision with respect of entry into the States of Sabah and Sarawak and the other provisions of this Agreement shall be conditional upon the enactment of the said Act.

Article VI

The Agreement on external defence and mutual assistance between the Government of the United Kingdom and the Government of the Federation of Malaya of 12th October, 1957, and its annexes shall apply to all territories of Malaysia, and any reference in that Agreement to the Federation of Malaya shall be deemed to apply to Malaysia, subject to the proviso that the Government of Malaysia will afford to the Government of the United Kingdom the right to continue to maintain the bases and other facilities at present occupied by their Service Authorities within the State of Singapore and will permit the Government of the United Kingdom to make such use of these bases and facilities as that Government may consider necessary for the purpose of assisting in the defence of Malaysia, and for the Commonwealth defence and for the preservation of peace in South-East Asia. The application of the said Agreement shall be subject to the provisions of Annex F to this Agreement (relating primarily to Service lands in Singapore).

Article VII

(1) The Federation of Malaya agrees that Her Britannic Majesty may make before Malaysia Day Orders in Council in the form set out in Annex G to this Agreement for the purpose of making provision for the payment of compensation and retirement benefits to certain overseas officers serving immediately before Malaysia Day, in the public service of the Colony of North Borneo or the Colony of Sarawak.

(2) On or as soon as practicable after Malaysia Day, public officer's agreements in the forms set out in annexes H and I of this Agreement shall be signed on behalf of the Government of the United Kingdom and the Government of Malaysia and the Government of Malaysia shall obtain the concurrence of the Government of the States of Sabah, Sarawak or Singapore, as the case may require, to the signature of the agreement by the Government of Malaysia so far as its terms may affect the responsibilities or interests of the Government of the State.

Article VIII

The Governments of the Federation of Malaya, North Borneo and Sarawak will take such legislative, executive or other action as may be required to implement the assurances, undertakings and recommendations contained in Chapter 3 of, and annexes A and B to, the report of the Inter-Governmental Committee signed on 27th February, 1963, in so far as they are not implemented by express provision of the Constitution of Malaysia.

Article IX

The provision of Annex J to this Agreement relating to Common Market and financial arrangements shall constitute an agreement between the Government of the Federation of Malaya and the Government of Singapore.

Article X

The Governments of the Federation of Malaya and of Singapore will take such legislative, executive or other action as may be required to implement the arrangements with respect to broadcasting and television set out in Annex K to this agreement in so far as they are not implemented by express provision of the Constitution of Malaysia.

Article XI

This agreement shall be signed in the English and Malay languages except that the annexes shall be in the English language only. In case of doubt the English text of the agreement shall prevail.

2

MANILA ACCORD

The Governments of the Federation of Malaya, the Republic of Indonesia and the Republic of the Philippines, prompted by their keen and common desire to have a general exchange of views on current problems concerning stability, security, economic development and social progress of the three countries and of the region and upon the initiative of President Diosdado Macapagal, agreed that a Conference of Ministers of the three countries be held in Manila on 7th June, 1963, for the purpose of achieving common understanding and close fraternal cooperation among themselves. Accordingly, Tun Abdul Razak, Deputy Prime Minister of the Federation of Malaya; Dr. Subandrio, Deputy First Minister/Minister for Foreign Affairs of the Republic of Indonesia; and Honourable Emmanuel Pelaez, Vice President of the Philippines and concurrently Secretary of Foreign Affairs, met in Manila from 7 to 11 June, 1963.

2. The deliberations were held in a frank manner and in a most cordial atmosphere in keeping with the spirit of friendship prevailing in the various meetings held between President Soekrano of the Republic of Indonesia, and Prime Minister Tunku Abdul Rahman Putra of the Federation of Malaya, and President Diosdado Macapagal. This Min-

isterial Conference was a manifestation of the determination of the nations in this region to achieve closer cooperation in their endeavour to chart their common future.

3. The Ministers were of one mind that the three countries share a primary responsibility for the maintenance of the stability and security of the area from subversion in any form or manifestation in order to preserve their respective national identities, and to ensure the peaceful development of their respective countries and of their region, in accordance with the ideals and aspirations of their peoples.

4. In the same spirit of common and constructive endeavour, they exchanged views on the proposed Confederation of nations of Malay origin, the proposed Federation of Malaysia, the Philippine claim to North Borneo and related problems.

The Macapagal Plan

5. Recognising that it is in the common interest of their countries to maintain fraternal relations and to strengthen cooperation among their peoples who are bound together by ties of race and culture, the three Ministers agreed to intensify the joint and individual efforts of their countries to secure lasting peace, progress and prosperity for themselves and for their neighbours.

6. In this context, the three Ministers supported President Macapagal's plan envisaging the grouping of the three nations of Malay origin working together in closest harmony but without surrendering any portion of their sovereignty. This calls for the establishment of the necessary common organs.

7. The three Ministers agreed to take the initial steps towards this ultimate aim by establishing machinery for frequent and regular consultations. The details of such machinery will be further defined. This machinery will enable the three Governments to hold regular consultations at all levels to deal with matters of mutual interest and concern consistent with the national, regional and international responsibilities or obligations of each country without prejudice to its sovereignty and independence. The Ministers agreed that their countries will endeavour to achieve close understanding and cooperation in dealing with common problems relating to security, stability, economic, social and cultural development.

8. In order to accelerate the process of growth towards the ultimate establishment of President Macapagal's plan, the Ministers agreed that each country shall set up its own National Secretariat. Pending the

establishment of a Central Secretariat for the consultative machinery, the National Secretaries should coordinate and cooperate with each other in the fulfilment of their tasks.

9. The Ministers further agreed to recommend that Heads of Government and Foreign Ministers meet at least once a year for the purpose of consultations on matters of importance and common concern.

Malaysia and North Borneo

10. The Ministers reaffirmed their countries' adherence to the principle of self-determination for the peoples of non-self-governing territories. In this context, Indonesia and the Philippines stated that they would welcome the formation of Malaysia provided the support of the people of the Borneo territories is ascertained by an independent and impartial authority, the Secretary-General of the United Nations or his representative.

11. The Federation of Malaya expressed appreciation for this attitude of Indonesia and the Philippines and undertook to consult the British Government and the Governments of the Borneo territories with a view to inviting the Secretary-General of the United Nations or his representative to take the necessary steps in order to ascertain the wishes of the people of those territories.

12. The Philippines made it clear that its position on the inclusion of North Borneo in the Federation of Malaysia is subject to the final outcome of the Philippine claim to North Borneo. The Ministers took note of the Philippine claim and the right of the Philippines to continue to pursue it in accordance with international law and the principle of the pacific settlement of disputes. They agreed that the inclusion of North Borneo in the Federation of Malaysia would not prejudice either the claim or any right thereunder. Moreover, in the context of their close association, the three countries agreed to exert their best endeavours to bring the claim to a just and expeditious solution by peaceful means, such as negotiation, conciliation, arbitration, or judicial settlement as well as other peaceful means of the parties' own choice, in conformity with the Charter of the United Nations and the Bandung Declaration.

13. In particular, considering the close historical ties between the peoples of the Philippines and North Borneo as well as their geographical propinquity, the Ministers agreed that in the event of North Borneo joining the proposed Federation of Malaysia the Government of the latter and the Government of the Philippines should maintain and promote

the harmony and the friendly relations subsisting in their region to ensure the security and stability of the area.

Meeting of Heads of Government

14. The Ministers agreed to recommend that a Meeting of their respective Heads of Government be held in Manila not later than the end of July 1963.

15. The Ministers expressed satisfaction over the atmosphere of brotherliness and cordiality which pervaded their Meeting and considered it as a confirmation of their close fraternal ties and as a happy augury for the success of future consultations among their leaders.

16. The Ministers agreed to place on record their profound appreciation of and gratitude for the statesmanlike efforts of President Macapagal whose courage, vision and inspiration not only facilitated the holding of this historic Meeting but also contributed towards the achievement for the first time of a unity of purpose and a sense of common dedication among the peoples of Malaya, Indonesia and the Philippines.

Approved and Accepted.

MANILA.

July 31, 1963

SOEKARNO,
President of the Republic of Indonesia

DIOSDADO MACAPAGAL,
President of the Philippines

TUNKU ABDUL RAHMAN PUTRA AL-HAJ,
Prime Minister of the Federation of Malaya

MANILA DECLARATION

The President of the Republic of Indonesia, the President of the Philippines and the Prime Minister of the Federation of Malaya, assembled in a Summit Conference in Manila from July 30 to August 5, 1963, following the Meeting of their Foreign Ministers held in Manila from June 7 to 11, 1963;

Conscious of the historic significance of their coming together for the first time as leaders of sovereign States that have emerged after long struggles from colonial status to independence;

Desiring to achieve better understanding and closer cooperation in their endeavour to chart their common future;

Inspired also by the spirit of Asian-African solidarity forged in the Bandung Conference of 1955;

Convinced that their countries, which are bound together by close historical ties of race and culture, share a primary responsibility for the maintenance of the stability and security of the area from subversion in any form or manifestation in order to preserve their respective national identities and to ensure the peaceful development of their respective countries and their region in accordance with the ideals and aspirations of their peoples; and

Determined to intensify the joint and individual efforts of their countries to secure lasting peace, progress and prosperity for themselves and their neighbours in a world dedicated to freedom and justice;

Do Hereby Declare

First, that they reaffirm their adherence to the principle of equal rights and self-determination of peoples as enunciated in the United Nations Charter and the Bandung Declaration;

Second, that they are determined, in the common interest of their countries, to maintain fraternal relations, to strengthen cooperation among their peoples in the economic, social and cultural fields in order to promote economic progress and social well-being in the region, and to put an end to the exploitation of man by man and of one nation by an other;

Third, that the three nations shall combine their efforts in the common struggle against colonialism and imperialism in all their forms and manifestations and for the eradication of the vestiges thereof in the region in particular and the world in general;

Fourth, that the three nations, as new emerging forces in the region, shall cooperate in building a new and better world based on national freedom, social justice and lasting peace; and

Fifth, that in the context of the joint endeavours of the three nations to achieve the foregoing objectives, they have agreed to take initial steps towards the establishment of Maphilindo by holding frequent and regular consultations at all levels to be known as Mushawarah Maphilindo.

MANILA,
August 5, 1963

SOEKARNO,
President of the Republic of Indonesia

DIOSDADO MACAPAGAL,
President of the Philippines

TUNKU ABDUL RAHMAN PUTRA AL-HAJ,
Prime Minister of Federation of Malaya

JOINT STATEMENT

The President of the Republic of Indonesia, the President of the Philippines, and the Prime Minister of the Federation of Malaya met at a summit conference in Manila from July 30 to August 5, 1963.

1. Moved by a sincere desire to solve their common problems in an atmosphere of fraternal understanding, they considered, approved and accepted the report and recommendations of the Foreign Ministers of the three countries adopted in Manila on June 11, 1963 (hereafter to be known as the Manila Accord).

2. In order to provide guiding principles for the implementation of the Manila Accord the Heads of Government have issued a declaration known as the Manila Declaration, embodying the common aspirations and objectives of the peoples and governments of the three countries.

3. As a result of the consultations amongst the three Heads of Government in accordance with the principles enunciated in the Manila Declaration, they have resolved various current problems of common concern.

4. Pursuant to paragraphs 10 and 11 of the Manila Accord the United Nations Secretary-General or his representative should ascertain prior to the establishment of the Federation of Malaysia the wishes of the people of Sabah (North Borneo) and Sarawak within the context of General Assembly Resolution 1541 (XV), Principle 9 of the Annex, by a fresh approach, which in the opinion of the Secretary-General is necessary to ensure complete compliance with the principle of self-determination within the requirements embodied in Principle 9, taking into consideration:

(I) the recent elections in Sabah (North Borneo) and Sarawak but nevertheless further examining, verifying and satisfying himself as to whether

(*a*) Malaysia was a major issue, if not the main issue;

(*b*) electoral registers were properly compiled;

(*c*) elections were free and there was no coercion; and

(*d*) votes were properly polled and properly counted; and

(II) the wishes of those who, being qualified to vote, would have exercised their right of self-determination in the recent elections had it not been for their detention for political activities, imprisonment for political offences or absence from Sabah (North Borneo) or Sarawak.

5. The Secretary-General will be requested to send working teams to carry out the task set out in paragraph 4.

6. The Federation of Malaya, having undertaken to consult the British Government and the Governments of Sabah (North Borneo) and Sarawak under paragraph 11 of the Manila accord on behalf of the three Heads of Government, further undertake to request them to cooperate with the Secretary-General and to extend to him the necessary facilities so as to enable him to carry out his task as set out in paragraph 4.

7. In the interest of the countries concerned, the three Heads of Government deem it desirable to send observers to witness the carrying out of the task to be undertaken by the working teams, and the Federation of Malaya will use its best endeavours to obtain the cooperation of the British Government and the Governments of Sabah (North Borneo) and Sarawak in furtherance of this purpose.

8. In accordance with paragraph 12 of the Manila Accord, the three Heads of Government decided to request the British Government to agree to seek a just and expeditious solution to the dispute between the British Government and the Philippine Government concerning Sabah (North Borneo) by means of negotiation, conciliation and arbitration, judicial settlement, or other peaceful means of the parties' own choice in conformity with the Charter of the United Nations. The three Heads of Government take cognizance of the position regarding the Philippine claim to Sabah (North Borneo) after the establishment of the Federation of Malaysia as provided under paragraph 12 of the Manila Accord, that is, that the inclusion of Sabah (North Borneo) in the Federation of Malaysia does not prejudice either the claim or any right thereunder.

9. Pursuant to paragraphs 6, 7, 8, and 9 of the Manila Accord and the fifth principle of the Manila Declaration, that is, that initial steps should be taken towards the establishment of Maphilindo by holding frequent and regular consultations at all levels to be known as Mushawarah

Maphilindo, it is agreed that each country shall set up a national secretariat for Maphilindo affairs and as a first step the respective national secretariats will consult together with a view to coordinating and cooperating with each other in the study on the setting up of the necessary machinery for Maphilindo.

10. The three Heads of Government emphasized that the responsibility for the preservation of the national independence of the three countries and of the peace and security in their region lies primarily in the hands of the governments and the peoples of the countries concerned, and that the three Governments undertake to have close consultations (Mushawarah) among themselves on these matters.

11. The three Heads of Government further agreed that foreign bases—temporary in nature—should not be allowed to be used directly or indirectly to subvert the national independence of any of the three countries. In accordance with the principle enunciated in the Bandung Declaration, the three countries will abstain from the use of arrangements of collective defence to serve the particular interests of any of the big powers.

12. President Sukarno and Prime Minister Tunku Abdul Rahman express their deep appreciation for the initiative taken by President Macapagal in calling the Summit Conference which, in addition to resolving their differences concerning the proposed Federation of Malaysia, resulted in paving the way for the establishment of Maphilindo. The three Heads of Government conclude this conference, which has greatly strengthened the fraternal ties which bind their three countries and extended the scope of their cooperation and understanding, with renewed confidence that their governments and peoples will together make a significant contribution to the attainment of just and enduring peace, stability and prosperity in the region.

MANILA,
August 5, 1963.

INDEX

Index